THE BATTERED WOMAN AND SHELTERS

SUNY Series in Deviance and Social Control

Ronald A. Farrell, Editor

THE BATTERED WOMAN AND SHELTERS

The Social Construction of Wife Abuse

Donileen R. Loseke

State University of New York Press

Published by
State University of New York Press, Albany

© 1992   State University of New York

For information, address the State University of New York Press,
State University Plaza, Albany, NY 12246

Production by Christine M. Lynch
Marketing by Fran Keneston

Library of Congress Cataloging-in-Publication Data

Loseke, Donileen R., 1947-
     The battered woman and shelters : the social construction of wife
abuse / Donileen R. Loseke.
          p.   cm. — (SUNY series in deviance and social control)
     Includes bibliographical references and index.
     ISBN 0-7914-0831-0. — ISBN 0-7914-0832-9 (pbk. : alk. paper)
     1. Social work with women—United States. 2. Abused women—United
States. 3. Women's shelters—United States. 4. Wife abuse—United
States. I. Title. II. Series.
HV1445.L67 1992
362.82'9285'0973—dc20
                                                                                    90-26166
                                                                                    CIP

10 9 8 7 6 5 4 3 2 1

CONTENTS

ACKNOWLEDGMENTS

I found compiling a list of acknowledgments to be a humbling task. I have more debts than I can acknowledge to people for their acts of kindness toward me and this project, to those who have read one or another part of my story and have given me intellectual assistance, and to those whose story I attempt to tell.

My debt is too large to neatly summarize for some people. Spencer Cahill, who, among other statuses, is my best friend and most trusted colleague, has listened to my talk about battered women and shelter work for all too many years. He has given me unending support; this project has benefited from his keen intellectual insights and his insistence that I tell the story in my data. I also cannot properly acknowledge my debt to the workers and clients of the South Coast shelter and its umbrella organization. They taught me to look at the lived realities of shelter work, they taught me that each victimized woman is a unique person and must be understood as such. They wanted me to tell their story. Although they must remain nameless, I have not forgotten their faces, nor have I forgotten Nancy who must be acknowledged for bringing the flowers. There also are many people who have given me support and who have given this project the benefits of their keen intellectual insights.

Don Zimmerman, Thomas Wilson, and Sarah Fenstermaker have given me advice for years and have wanted me to tell the story in my data. Gale Miller, James Holstein, Norman Denzin, Gary Alan Fine, Robert Emerson and Joel Best each have offered insights, which have been critical in the development of this perspective. I am indebted to Demie Kurz for the same reason and also for her political judgments and emotional sensitivity. Finally, without the encouragement of Ronald Farrell, I would not have written this. I am grateful for the support and assistance of these people and many others. I hope the story I tell reflects the support I have received.

Introduction:

Social Problems Work and the Study of Wife Abuse

All situations that are experienced by people as painful do not become matters of public activity and targets for public action . . . "Objective" conditions are seldom so compelling and so clear in their form that they spontaneously generate a "true" consciousness.

Joseph Gusfield, *The Culture of Public Problems*

As fast as new medical categories . . . were invented . . . new kinds of people spontaneously came forward in hoards to accept the labels and to live accordingly . . . new names are uttered and forthwith new creatures corresponding to them emerge.

Mary Douglas, *How Institutions Think*

In the mid-1970s, three new social categories appeared in America. One category labeled a new social problem—"wife abuse," one labeled a new type of person—"battered woman," and one labeled a new type of social service—"shelters for the battered woman." Between then and now, hundreds of books, articles, and social service training manuals have been written about the characteristics of this type of problem, person, and social service; volumes of statistics have been produced demonstrating that wife abuse is a life-threatening problem, that the battered woman is a worthy and needy social service recipient, and that shelters are life saving services for such a woman. Given this, the first question is obvious: Why do we need yet another study of these topics?

This work differs from most of the existing literature on these topics. Rather than constituting wife abuse and the battered woman as the subjects for study, I am interested in these as *objects* that are socially

1

constructed. Like Joseph Gusfield, my interest is in understanding how a world of reality is socially constructed; like Mary Douglas, my interest is in the social processes whereby we define and then create particular "types of creatures." Stated otherwise, I am interested in the social process behind what Ian Hacking has called "making up people."[1]

This analysis lies in the social construction tradition of the study of public problems. In this tradition, social problems and deviance designations are not assumed to be mirrors or reflections of objective conditions. They rather are understood to be the results of human activity. Questions about *how* social problems emerge have obvious validity for the problem now called "wife abuse." As documented by many observers, the historical records clearly show that the behaviors of husbands assaulting their wives have been present throughout history, yet only from time to time do these behaviors receive public attention. When "wife abuse" emerged in the 1970s as a public problem, it was not because the condition was new. Rather, it took claims-making activities to define this condition as a public problem and this required convincing the general public that the behaviors we now call "wife abuse" were morally intolerable and that women we now call "battered women" required and deserved public sympathy.

The social construction approach often focuses on examining the activities leading to new public consciousness that specific conditions should be accorded the status of a public problem. But this already has been done for the problem now called "wife abuse." Many observers maintain simply that this social problem consciousness is the result of activists in the amorphous "battered woman's movement," a movement, in turn, often credited to the general "woman's movement." Within these arguments, feminist consciousness-raising groups are acknowledged for leading individual women to awareness that their personal experiences of victimization were shared by others; feminist activists are credited for coining the term "battered woman," and for creating the first shelters for such a woman.[2] In brief, much already is known about how wife abuse entered public consciousness. What remains to be examined?

I want to expand the focus of the social construction perspective by following the lead of James Holstein and Gale Miller who argue that the traditional focus on "claims-making activities" leading to new social problem consciousness is too narrow. As important as it is to understand the political processes surrounding the initial construction of social problems, that does not exhaust the myriad questions about "social problems work," which they define as all the human activity "implicated in the recognition, identification, interpretation and definition of conditions called social problems."[3] So, I will be examining wife abuse and the battered woman as they are examples of Durkheimian collective representations, which are publicly standardized cultural categorization systems, and as they are examples of what Alfred Schutz calls "schemes of interpretation" which are frameworks for organizing and making sense of practical experience.[4] As socially constructed, the collective representation of wife abuse is a system for categorizing violence and for morally evaluating it; as constructed, the battered woman is a collective representation for a woman with a particular type of experience, biography, motivation, and subjectivity. My concern is with the specific content of these categorizations and with how they are used by frontline workers at a shelter for the battered woman. Since any particular collective representation is only one of myriad possible ways to make sense of experience, it follows that my analysis will be messy. While I will illustrate several types of social problems work involved in the production and reproduction of the public problem called "wife abuse," I also will not paint an image of this work as clear, straightforward, or deterministic.

My first two chapters begin this reflexive analysis by considering dimensions of public categorization systems. Chapter 1 examines the specific content of these representations as they have been publicly constructed. Using academic journal articles, transcripts of public policy hearings, and mass media magazine articles as my texts, I will argue that wife abuse and the battered woman are labels for collective representations with very specific contents, and that these specific contents furnish warrants for a particular type of social service—shelters for the battered woman.

As collective representations, wife abuse and the battered woman can be used as interpretive devices. In chapter 2, I will examine the underlying moral dimensions to wife abuse and the battered woman and then I will turn to the issue of using these categorization systems as interpretive devices. Within the complexities, heterogeneity, and ambiguities of lived realities, events and persons do not come to us prelabeled and that is my question: What must be subjectively apprehended about an individual experience in order to classify it as one of "wife abuse?" What must be subjectively apprehended about an individual woman in order to classify her as a "battered woman?" This chapter first examines the collective representations of wife abuse and the battered woman in relation to the cultural schemes surrounding the moral evaluation of violence and the moral evaluation of sympathy worthiness. Certainly, I am not denying the importance of examining wife abuse within the framework of sexism; my story is not offered to challenge the many claims that wife abuse can be understood only within the framework of sexism and women's inequality. But I will argue that the cultural schemes of interpretation surrounding the moral evaluation of violence and the moral evaluation of people likewise are critical because both influence the process whereby social members accept, understand, and use these collective representations as interpretive devices to make sense of practical experience.

After examining wife abuse and the battered woman representations as they are interpretive devices available to social members in general, I will turn to looking at social problems work at one shelter which I will call "South Coast." Chapter 3 begins this examination by considering how the organizers of this place translated collective representations of what shelters should do into organizational form, rules, and methods of service provision. But this translation of collective ideals into organizational form was accomplished within myriad practical constraints so South Coast definitely could not be portrayed as an exemplar of the ideal form of shelters for the battered woman. Nonetheless, the organization was the immediate site for the social problems work of front-line workers, the persons actually charged with helping the battered woman.

Chapter 4 then examines the worker activity of selecting shelter clients. This task of client selection at South Coast was accomplished within the contexts of organizational practicalities and conflicting moralities. While decisions were made by folk reasoning, workers nonetheless displayed to one another in their formal accounting that women allowed entry were of the "battered woman" type, that women denied entry were of the "not-battered" type. This is the social problems work of allowing only some women to become official members of the battered woman social collectivity.

Although workers could rhetorically construct all clients as specific instances of the battered woman, chapter 5 begins with the fact that such rhetorical constructions did not reduce client heterogeneity, nor was the experience of a shelter stay sufficient to transform clients from instances of a battered woman to instances of a "strong and independent woman," the goal of shelter services. This chapter then examines how the organizationally sponsored interpretive scheme and the structural arrangements at South Coast allowed and encouraged workers to actively intervene in clients' lives in ways justified as necessary and good for women of the battered woman type.

Chapter 6 concludes my examination of social problems work at South Coast by turning to the troubles in this place. Although the collective representation of the battered woman would lead us to expect that such a woman would be a good and grateful client and that services would successfully transform her into a different type of person, this was not always the case at South Coast. Workers here could construct some clients as very demanding, troublesome, complaining, and ungrateful; it also was difficult for workers to see many objective and positive results of their efforts on behalf of clients. Yet workers at this place could—at times—neutralize these troubles by modifying the collective representation of the battered woman in ways salvaging the meaning of shelter work, and in ways neutralizing troubles of all sorts. This examination, though, also illustrates the limits of this device in neutralizing worker frustration, the reliance of this device on folk reasoning, and the tendency of this device to rhetorically transform clients into "hopeless creatures."

These three chapters, examining worker practical activity at one shelter, show aspects of the social problems work of using collective representations as interpretive devices within the messiness of lived reality and within organizationally imposed limitations. When taken together, this analysis shows the process of "making up people" in human service organizations—the process of transforming heterogeneity into homogeneity, of constructing a type of person out of the raw confusion of practical experience, of reproducing the social collectivities of "wife abuse" and the "battered woman."

My data for this analysis come from one shelter. Some data, explained more fully in the appendix, come from formal interviews with workers and administrators, weekly staff meetings, and formal agency documents. Most of the relevant data, though, are not from such formal sources and rather come from my participant observation and from the shelter "logbook," an ongoing, worker written, running commentary on life inside South Coast. These data furnish a behind-the-scenes view of this organization, an insider's view of how workers built and shared a common culture, a view of how they used the documentary method of interpretation, which relied on their understandings of "wife abuse" and the "battered woman," while simultaneously reproducing those understandings.[5]

This raises another question: Who am I to have such insider's data? Often I have wished I could write a brief and methodologically correct paragraph explaining my role in this organization. Originally, I entered South Coast as an evaluator working for its umbrella organization. My job had little to do with the shelter, and for the first few months, I simply tabulated statistics on the number of clients served. Although this did not get me close to actual shelter work, simply being there pulled me into participation. This was a loosely structured organization, to say the least, and they always needed volunteer help. I remember the day my role there was transformed. As usual, I went to check the records but the one on duty worker had to leave to take a client somewhere. The phone rang and I knew I had two choices: I could continue my work (and perhaps note that a call had gone unanswered), or I could answer the phone. I did not want to answer it. What did I know? I was merely a graduate student and all I knew about shelter work was what I had read in a few academic articles and what I had heard in a few staff meetings. But the phone ring was compelling and I answered it. When the worker returned, she was pleased because, according to her, I was now a bona fide shelter worker.

Over the next two years or so the ebb and flow of my involvement at South Coast depended on my own work schedule and on the needs of the organization. I would retreat into my university office for days or weeks at a time. Once, I reemerged to find a totally new group of workers had replaced the ones I knew; many clients came and went during my absences. At other times, especially when one or another problem caused a shortage of workers, I did considerable volunteering. Most of it was mundane: I accompanied clients to court and transported them around town on various errands; I watched children so clients and workers could have uninterrupted support groups; I picked up donations of food and clothing, I helped organize a rummage sale, and so on. During one time, though, the organization lost most of its funding and I did serve as a worker, primarily handling calls received from midnight to 8:00 A.M. Although this was almost a decade ago, these experiences still are vivid in my memory: Sitting in a restaurant at 2:00 A.M. listening to a woman talk about her myriad troubles; helping a woman remove her belongings from her home while a police officer stood by to restrain her angry spouse; the hospital emergency room at 1:00 A.M. on New Year's day; thinking to myself a woman was in incredible danger while listening to her explain why it was quite impossible for her to leave her home; a 4:00 A.M. call from a woman who lived forty-five miles away, who was quite insistent that I come get her and her five children and then take them back at 8:00 A.M. Complexity, horror, indeterminancy, confusion, frustration—what I most recall about the substance of shelter work at South Coast.

So, I am claiming that my personal experiences inform my analysis. But I am not claiming that I ever was a true shelter worker. I always had the nonworker privilege of determining what I would do and when I would do it; I simply refused to do some things such as take part in decisions to exile troublesome clients. Furthermore, although I talked with many women who used South Coast services and although I maintained contact with a few of them for several months, I always identified myself honestly as a graduate student, researcher, and volunteer. So, unlike true workers at this place, shelter work was not my employment responsibility, or my occupational identity; the shelter was not my employment site.

My continuing and multifaceted involvement with this place raises questions about the validity of my data but again, I have no simple and methodologically correct response. From time to time, I will be able to compare my data with those collected at other shelters, and this will allow readers to judge consistency of my data with others. But data bias primarily is mediated by the fact that, while I was at South Coast, I was not pursuing my current theoretical interests in social problems work and the reflexive relationships among social collectivity images, commonsense interpretive structures, and worker practical activity. True, I did complete my dissertation while I was there and it was about the practice of shelter work. But my focus then was in describing the practical disjunctures between theory and practice. No doubt due to my own experiences and to the fact that I personally saw South Coast workers as people with good intentions, my interest then was to offer alternatives to the academic and social movement literature, which tends to portray frontline workers in places such as South Coast as somehow individually responsible for disappointing differences between the theory and the practice of social services. I wish I had my present set of questions while I was still at South Coast. My data for this analysis would have been better and, for that matter, so would have been my dissertation.

It was later when I started teaching courses in the sociology of family violence that I began to look at all my data as part of a larger story. On the first day of class, I always ask students to anonymously write questions they would like answered during the semester. Invariably, the most common questions are definitional. They want to know, for example, "What, precisely, counts as wife abuse?" "Does it count if my mom is an alcoholic and my dad has to slap her when she's out of control?" "How do I know if someone is a battered woman?" In reviewing my shelter field notes one day for an unrelated project, I was amazed at how often new South Coast workers had posed these same questions of definitional boundaries. Just as Kathleen Ferraro has noted that new workers at another shelter experienced confusion and looked to more seasoned workers for guidelines,[6] new South Coast workers wanted more experienced workers to tell them what "counts" as "wife abuse." My students and new shelter workers, it seems, believe there are boundaries to this public problem.

It was then that I began to think about the implications of the fact that collective representations such as wife abuse and the battered woman are socially constructed. They are not folk categorizations arising from practical experience, yet they nonetheless are mediated by commonsense interpretive structures. This all leads to complexity and confusion. My students, for example, are often deeply concerned about the public problem of wife abuse, but according to them, behaviors such as "slapping," "pushing," or "shoving" are *not* wife abuse. My students are deeply concerned about the battered woman, yet they persist in withholding this label from any woman who in any way can be seen as implicated in the production of her victimization. Now I understand the constant arguments I have with my students over such distinctions to be the key to the case: Their implicit, commonsense distinctions are the same as those made by South Coast workers. And, of course, distinctions made by social service workers have many consequences. It is worker practical activity in places such as South Coast that determines which women will and which women will not be allowed entry and thus become official members of the social collectivity called "battered woman"; it is worker practical activity that shapes some women—rhetorically if not in fact—into a type of person seeable as a battered woman; it is worker activity that reproduces collective representations such as "wife abuse" and the "battered woman"; it is worker activity that repairs disjunctures between the homogeneity of collective images and the heterogeneity of lived realities. Bluntly stated, the answers to my students' questions—what is "wife abuse" and who is the "battered woman"—are decided by social problems work.

This topic of social problems work is about the activity of creating collective representations, of using representations to evaluate practical experience; it is about producing and reproducing social problems. As such, this study is about the social problems industry surrounding the public problem we now call "wife abuse."[7] Throughout this work and particularly in the conclusion, I will be emphasizing how this social problems industry reflects characteristics of modern day America. In many ways, wife abuse and the battered woman are merely case examples demonstrating general cultural characteristics—what types of situations Americans define as troublesome and what types of people we define as worthy of help. In the final analysis, wife abuse and the battered woman exemplify the social problems work of producing and reproducing collective images and thereby producing and reproducing social structure.

In many ways, the issues for this analysis differ from those more common in the examination of social problems. My concern here is not with the objective reality of wife abuse; it is with how this public problem has been socially constructed. So, rather than offering readers the overwhelming evidence for why violence against women *is* a social problem, I will focus on how some violence—and only some violence—has been labeled as that of "wife abuse." Rather than telling my readers about the dire situations and problems of women victims of violence, I will examine how some characteristics—and only some characteristics—of women have been characterized as those of a "battered woman." My questions, in brief, are of a different sort than those usually associated with the social problem now called "wife abuse." Yet *clearly and most certainly*, while I am bracketing the objective realities of violence toward women, I do not deny that it is all too common for women to be victimized in their homes. This has been repeatedly demonstrated. In my opinion, the force of arguments and evidence constituting violence against women as a social problem *cannot be denied*. I begin, therefore, by assuming my readers believe as I do that violence against women is an all too common feature of American life. At the same time, a careful reader may have noticed a shift in terminology. It is a social fact, an objective, empirical reality that women are the victims of violence. But why is it that only some of this violence and only some of these women victims have become topics of public concern? Why only some forms of violence? Why only some women? Why and how does it matter that wife abuse and the battered woman have been socially constructed out of the raw confusions of lived realities? These are my practical questions.

This analysis should not be read as a criticism of claims-makers and social service providers who have socially constructed wife abuse and the battered woman. On the contrary, my major point is that these specific constructions are the only viable ones in modern day America, and that workers' practices are logical and common sense. But certainly, there *are* practical implications of the social problems work surrounding these categories. This work no doubt has assisted women whose experiences and characteristics more or less conform to public images but who has been left out? Do women need to buy their way into emergency social services by proving themselves to be victims? Do women need to show their bruises and broken bones to receive public sympathy? Do women need to act like a battered woman—a poor, defenseless, helpless creature—in order to secure needed housing? What about a woman who wants assistance *before* she is subjected to extreme violence, *before* she is a battered woman? Where is the sympathy for her? How do our public categorizations prevent women from seeking *and* receiving early assistance? In the final chapter, I will address these issues—the very real practical implications of the typical answers to the questions, "what is wife abuse?" and "who is the battered woman?" What may seem esoteric and academic—the social construction of reality—has real implications for real women. They are my practical concern.

Chapter One

Collective Representations

Human problems do not spring up, full-blown and announced
into the consciousness of bystanders. Even to recognize a situation as painful requires a system for categorizing and defining
events.

Joseph Gusfield, *The Culture of Public Problems*

My first task is to examine the content of the collective representations of wife abuse and the battered woman and to illustrate how these
particular representations furnish a mandate for a particular type of
social service: shelters. Certainly, the terms "wife abuse" and the "battered woman" have entered public consciousness, but what do these
labels mean? What is their content?

My wish to deconstruct claims forming these new collective representations is not easy to achieve for several reasons. First, claims formulating these representations have been made on many stages of social
problem construction such as in academic and mass media publications,
in public policy hearings and in trade journals for social service
providers. Obviously, the form of discourse varies according to writer
and audience. Second, claims have been advanced by a variety of persons who do not share a common discourse; no authority is invested in
any one person or group. Indeed, although wife abuse has been publicly
labeled as a "woman's issue," not all claims-makers advance themselves
as feminists, and there are recurring debates and disagreements among
those who *do* identify themselves as feminist.[1] Third, my hope to deconstruct the content of these claims is made even more difficult by the fact
that few claims even contain explicit definitions.

Since my interest is in the collective representations that have drifted into public consciousness, I will cast a wide net so that I can look at claims made by academic psychologists, sociologists, and historians, by self-proclaimed feminist activists and by social service providers on all stages of social problem construction. Since I believe that any one claim is not all that important, I will bracket issues often of interest to academics. In particular, I will not examine nuances of differences among claims. Most certainly, claims-makers have not spoken with a united voice and the academic literature is filled with often contentious debates among them. Yet for my project, these debates *are* "academic" and of little interest to the general public. My concern, then, is with the general images, the public content of social problems rather than with the intricate theoretical frameworks sometimes underlying such images.

My data for this examination of the content of collective representations first of all include all seventy-seven articles referenced in the *Readers' Guide to Periodical Literature*, beginning with the first reference under a new heading, "wife abuse," appearing in 1974, and ending with articles published in 1986.[2] Furthermore, over the past decade I have collected texts of public policy hearings, academic journal articles, feminist publications, and social service manuals. While my bookcases and file cabinets are stuffed with this ever-expanding collection, I do not claim to have all treatments—the social problems industry surrounding this public problem is too large. So, I will leave it to the readers to decide whether or not I make my case about the content of these collective representations constructed through social problems claims-making.[3]

The collective representation of wife abuse

> But a domestic spat is not battering, which involves a pattern of escalating abuse in a situation from which the victim feels she cannot escape.
>
> *Time*, "Wife Beating"

> Wife beating...is a pattern of physical abuse of a woman at the hands of her former husband, husband, or male companion. It consists of repeated blows with the intention of inflicting harm.

It is more serious than a mere dispute and it is not a single shove or a single slap.

Marjory Fields, "Testimony"

What, specifically, *is* "wife abuse?" I will begin with three constructions agreed upon by almost all claims-makers. The first is that this condition is *not* limited to any specific group of women. Indeed, since claims-makers often define "wives" to include women in *any* cross-sex relationship, and since the labels "wife abuse/woman abuse" and "battered wife/battered woman" are used interchangeably, as constructed, wife abuse is not limited to women who are married.[4] Likewise, according to claims, this condition is not limited to any specific racial, social class, or ethnic group. This claim often is made by illustrating wife abuse with stories involving highly educated and/or affluent white women. Such women are called upon to tell their stories in public policy hearings; magazine readers are told "money in the bank or an expensive car is no guarantee against violence"; these stories have titles such as "Powerless in the Suburbs." Although claims-makers argue that wife abuse is not limited to women with particular demographic characteristics, they have paid *particular* attention to incorporating educated and affluent white women into the category of women experiencing this problem.[5]

Second, according to all claims-makers, "wife abuse" is a label for acts where women are the *pure victims*. This means that this condition is different from "mutual combat" where violence is jointly produced. While it is not common for claims-makers to make this distinction explicit, it is common for them to maintain simply that mutual combat is not a valid construction. This is accomplished by claiming that a woman, ipso facto is not violent, and/or that a woman's violence is limited to "self-defense."[6] Also as clearly, claims construct wife abuse as events that are not "victim precipitated." Ideas that a victimized woman somehow deserves to be victimized because she is too bossy, too nagging, too domineering, or too anything are routinely labeled as "pure myth." As constructed, wife abuse is about those events where a woman is a victim.[7]

Third, claims-makers agree that men are *offenders*. Here, too, claims invariably construct such a man as one found in any walk of life and here, too, illustrations often involve a man who is white and affluent. According to such claims, although such a man might appear quite normal in public—or even, as one magazine claimed, "slick and charming"—inside his home he is simply a brute or a monster.[8] Furthermore, claims-makers agree that such a man intends the violence he produces; "wife abuse" is not a label for "accidental" violence. It is formally defined as behavior by a man "in order to coerce her to do something he wants her to do without any concern for her rights"; such men are explicitly defined as men who "use violence in order to control and dominate their wives"; magazine readers are told "wife abuse is a pattern of coercive control, done by men who need to control women," and that it happens when "wives do not do what their husbands want them to do." This claim about men's intentionality to produce women as victims most often is advanced through stories labeled as "illustrating the condition." For example, in one magazine article, a woman told of being slapped and pushed to the floor when she did not cook a meal fast enough, another woman told of experiencing a bruising pinch whenever she voiced an opinion not shared by her husband. In her book, *The Battered Woman*, Lenore Walker tells the story of Anne, a woman who had been threatened with violence if she did not marry her husband, who had been thrown across a room because she had lunch with a woman friend he did not like, and who had been slammed against the wall because she asked her husband to drive her to work.[9] Of course, all such illustrations promote claims that wife abuse is not accidental, while simultaneously and graphically illustrating that a woman is a pure victim and a man is an offender.

In summary, most claims-makers construct wife abuse as a phenomenon crossing all demographic lines which involves men as offenders who intend to do harm and women as victims who do not create their victimization. These are the actors and motivations encompassed by the label, "wife abuse." But what, exactly, is "abuse?" This is an evaluative, not a behavioral term.

Some claims-makers argue that abuse should be defined broadly to include *any* behavior in which women are controlled by men.[10] But in their emphases and illustrations, most claims-makers construct wife abuse to be primarily about *physical violence*. It is explicitly defined in terms such as the "use of physical force," a "physical assault," or a "physical attack." Since wife abuse is defined in terms such as "real and serious physical assault," or "savage abuse," such events of physical violence are particularly those seeable as *extreme*. As defined by one policy maker, wife abuse is a label for a "good, harsh, brutal beating up."[11]

This content of wife abuse as extreme violence is found most often in claims-makers' illustrations. At a 1978 policy hearing in California, for example, policy makers heard about a woman whose husband first broke her neck and then followed her to the hospital where he tried to kill her; at the United States Commission on Civil Rights, policy makers heard about a woman who first was stabbed and then was thrown out of a second story window.[12] Expectably, mass media magazines also promote a brutal image of this condition. To take an example from *Readers Digest*:

> In the final beating . . . the wife was stabbed repeatedly . . . The husband then stomped on his wife's face and ran inside the house. He returned with their young son, and in front of the young boy, cursed and kicked the woman in the head.[13]

Such extreme images of the behaviors encompassed by the label, "wife abuse," are not limited to public policy hearings and mass media magazines. They also figure prominently in books about this subject. Popular books such as Del Martin's *Battered Wives*, Lenore Walker's *The Battered Woman*, and Mildred Pagelow's *Woman Battering*, each open with long personal stories demonstrating the extent of depravity encompassed by the label "wife abuse."[14] To take one example, *Battered Wives* begins with a "Letter from a Battered Woman." This woman says of her experiences:

> I have had glasses thrown at me. I have been kicked in the abdomen when I was visibly pregnant. I have been kicked off the bed and hit while lying on the floor—again while I was pregnant. I have been whipped, kicked, and thrown, picked up again and thrown down again. I have been punched and kicked in the head, chest, face, and abdomen more times than I can count.[15]

My point here is simple: While claims-makers often give a nod toward condemning all forms of violence, their claims construct the core of wife abuse to contain *extreme physical violence*. As explicitly defined and as implicitly illustrated, "wife abuse" is not "just slapping or shoving," it is not the same as a "marital quarrel," a "domestic spat," or a "domestic disturbance." According to claims, wife abuse is a label for events seeable as those of "conjugal terrorism."[16]

While less extreme physical violence lies somewhere outside the core of this social problem, wife abuse can be expanded to include *emotional violence*. This is sensible given the common sense assumption that emotional violence would accompany physical abuse. In the popular press, this is the claim that "between beatings he controls her with shouting, name calling, intimidation, and other emotional blows"; in public policy hearings it is the claim that wife abuse is a label for a constellation of behaviors which "may include being knocked down stairs and being demeaned and debased."[17] Although not as common, wife abuse also can be constructed to include emotional abuse occurring without physical assault. But when such nonphysical abuse stands alone, it typically is constructed as "severe," or, as Lenore Walker told policy makers, the problem is "life-threatening" emotional abuse.[18] Stories labeled as those of wife abuse in magazine articles illustrate that the content of emotional abuse is not a run-of-the-mill domestic problem: A man pouring gasoline on his wife's naked body and then flicking matches around her, a woman locked into her bedroom every day without any clothes and with the door handle wired with electricity to prevent her from escaping naked into the street, and a woman whose husband threatened to lock her into a coffin-like box he had built specifically for that purpose.[19]

For sensitive readers, I no doubt have lingered too long in describing the severity of acts labeled as those of wife abuse.[20] But this is the critical core of the collective representation and my point is that this core image is of brutalities and atrocities. The claim that wife abuse is a social problem is further supported by three other characteristics.

First, the label, "wife abuse," is not really a label for an event, per se, since it is defined explicitly as a *pattern* of physical abuse, or as a continuing *series* of abusive and degrading acts.[21] Thus, as constructed, wife abuse is a label for a series of events and hence a "battered woman" is explicitly defined as a woman who has been "systematically and severely beaten by her husband for many years."[22] As explicitly constructed, then, wife abuse is not a label for an "occasional slap." Furthermore, as constructed, this series of events is characterized by their *increasing severity and frequency*.[23] Still further, these events are characterized as *unstoppable*. True, after a violent event, an abusive man might feel guilty, he might act loving, contrite, and charming to this victim, but wife abuse is about those events where he *will* return to his abusive behavior. This claim is logical given the construction of the type of man who engages in wife abuse. While claims-makers complain that little research has focused on the characteristics of such a man, they also claim that a man guilty of wife abuse is one who believes abusing a woman is his right, and/or one who consistently denies the troublesome nature of his behavior. Given such an image, it follows that the prognosis for his change is poor indeed. So, claims construct wife abuse as increasingly frequent and severe behaviors that will not stop. Magazine readers are told simply "violence often starts mildly with a push, a shove, a slap. If no one interferes, it grows worse."[24] Most certainly, no claims-maker argues that one act of violence is acceptable, but it remains that in their emphases and explicit definitions, wife abuse is about *continuing, escalating*, and *unstoppable* victimization.

The next characteristic of wife abuse is not surprising and follows from other claims about the content of this social problem: Wife abuse is a label for acts producing *physical injury*. As explicitly defined, it is a label for acts yielding "severe, repeated, and demonstrable injury," for acts where women are subjected to "serious and/or repeated physical injury as a result of deliberate assaults." Indeed, one claims-maker even specified an expected degree of injury when she claimed that "severe bruising" was the "minimal injury" for acts of wife abuse.[25] Most commonly, this characteristic is not explicitly defined because it is to be expected that the kinds of violence encompassed by the label would produce injury. So, most commonly, claims about injuries are advanced through personal stories. For example, the "Letter From a Battered Woman" opening Del Martin's book is a story of a woman who experienced "painful bruises, swelling, bleeding wounds, and unconsciousness";[26] magazines contain stories about a woman who suffered a "ruptured spleen, broken bones and ribs," and another who "reached the hospital emergency room with a puffed and purple face, blood flowing from her ear, and two broken ribs."[27] Given that claims-makers on all stages of social problem construction frequently cite statistics on the number of women *killed* by wife abuse, it is clear that this is a label for acts producing *physical injury.*

●   The final characteristic of wife abuse follows from all others. As constructed, this is a label for acts perceived by victims to be *terrifying.* Explicitly and implicitly, wife abuse is not "masochistic" violence or "playful" violence. Indeed, it is anthetical to such constructions since magazine articles have titles such as "If You Loved Me, You Wouldn't Hurt Me," and "I Don't Want to be a Battered Wife." In brief, the label, "wife abuse," labels acts experienced by its victims as *terrifying.* Hence, women experiencing this tell of "Life in a Domestic Hell," and they talk of "Being an Abused Wife and Living in Fear."[28]

    When combined, these claims constitute the collective representation of the public problem we now call "wife abuse." In the composite image, wife abuse is a label for severe, frequent, and continuing violence that escalates over time and is unstoppable. Such violence is that in which unrepentant men intentionally harm women and where women are not the authors of their own experiences which they find terrifying.

    Such a collective representation was successful in overcoming popular public interpretations that violence by husbands against wives was not serious, was victim-precipitated and limited to poor and/or minority women. In defining such traditional interpretations as "myths of wife abuse," what had been previously interpreted as personal troubles were transformed into a public problem.[29] At the same time, the construction raises its own question: Why is such abuse repeated?

●   Of course, asking why abuse is repeated could be transformed into a question about men who abuse: Why does such a man persist in such despicable behavior? But the public and claims-makers alike have transformed this question about repeated behaviors into one about women victims: Why do they stay? After all, by definition, women victims are terrified of their abuse, which is extreme and repeated and consequential and only grows worse over time. Since the prognosis that a man will change is poor, it is justified for claims-makers to label a woman's hope for such change as a "false and futile dream." The collective representation of wife abuse leads to the common sense conclusion that a woman *should* leave such a relationship, and this prescription is a part of the collective representation: A woman experiencing wife abuse must leave her relationship. Within claims, a failure to leave is labeled as "maladaptive choice behavior," or as "self-destruction through inactivity"; social policy makers are told that the goal of policy should be to "help the battered woman leave the situation," that the issue is "how can we help her to leave"; social service providers tell one another that they should work to "effect permanent separation," and to help such a woman "terminate the relationship."[30]

It is not surprising that claims-makers have devoted considerable attention to answering the question, "why does she stay?"[31] If wife abuse is to be publicly accepted as a social problem then the behavior of staying in a relationship containing wife abuse must be constructed in a way not challenging claims about the content of this social problem. In other words, if a woman stays because violence is not "that bad," if she stays because she does not mind the abuse, indeed, if she stays because she *chooses* to stay for any reason, then claims about the content of this public problem are challenged. In the process of accounting for a woman's behavior of staying in a relationship containing wife abuse, claims construct a new type of person—a "battered woman"—a woman whose unexpectable behavior of staying in a relationship containing wife abuse supports rather than challenges claims about the content of this public problem.

The collective representation of the battered woman

Women stay with men who abuse them because of factors such as: fear; helplessness; guilt and feelings of failure; lack of resources signified by lack of freedom of movement, economic dependency and dependent children.

Mildred Pagelow, Family Violence

Battered women are often trapped: They lack the money to escape with their children, cannot earn a living and have lost hope of regaining control of their lives. And many hide the fact that they are abused in order to preserve the family unit.

Glamour, "Scarred Lives of Battered Women"

Without exception, the construction of the battered woman type of person begins with the obvious: She is a woman experiencing violence of the type known as "wife abuse." As such, her behavior of staying in her relationship ipso facto is defined as "unreasonable." Further, with few exceptions, the construction of the battered woman begins with an attribution: Her unreasonable behavior is not her fault. Claims formulating the battered woman construct her as a type of person who *is* deviant—she engages in unreasonable and unexpectable behavior—yet she is a woman who does not freely choose to be deviant. Claims construct this type of person through common sense and stereotypical associations to the social positions of wife/mother, woman, and victim.

Most commonly, claims-makers describe a battered woman as a stereotypical and traditional *wife* who has been economically dependent on her abuser and who has little opportunity to be otherwise. The characteristic of economic dependency is the most common term used to describe this type of woman and, according to almost all claims, this characteristic excuses her behavior of staying. Simply stated by one such woman who told her story in a magazine article:

> What am I supposed to do? Where am I going to go? I don't have any money and I don't know how to do anything. You tell me: Just what am I supposed to do when he beats me up?[32]

Furthermore, the majority of claims construct a battered woman as a *mother* with small children. This characteristic of motherhood serves to magnify the characteristic of economic dependency:

> Why does she not leave? The answer is simple. If she has children but no money and no place to go, she has no choice.[33]

We have a powerful image here of a type of woman who obviously does not choose to remain in her abusive relationship. When such a woman does attempt to leave, she is described as "the wife who grabs her children and flees her violent husband in the middle of the night . . ."[34] Or, as described by Senator Hatch in Congressional testimony:

> When a battered woman makes the decision to leave her husband, she may be in fear of her life. She commonly has nothing but the clothes on her back and the children she is afraid to leave with a violent spouse. For all too many of these women, there is no place to go.[35]

Most typically, the collective representation of the battered woman has at its core a wife/mother who remains within her abuse only because she has no place to go. But a careful reader might recall that the condition called "wife abuse" is constructed as a phenomenon crossing all social boundaries. Are affluent women also trapped by economic dependence? According to claims, many such women *are* trapped because their present affluence depends on their connections with affluent men. Indeed, claims-makers argue that an affluent woman might perceive even greater economic entrapment than a poor woman since she has a "long way to fall" if she leaves her partner.[36]

A critical reader, though, might still wonder whether or not such a collective representation of the battered woman is sufficient to account for the behavior of staying. For example, would not friends offer a woman a place to go to escape her abuse? According to claims—no. First, a battered woman is constructed as a woman isolated from others. Such isolation might be self-imposed since she is constructed as a type of woman who is "embarrassed over her plight," or isolation might be imposed by her partner as a "technique of control." Second, even if she is not isolated from others, claims-makers argue that such a woman should not expect any assistance. Her friends might perceive themselves to be in danger if they help; since an abusive man often appears normal, her friends might not believe her stories of brutality; they might not be familiar with the characteristics of wife abuse and believe she created her own victimization. In brief, a battered woman is constructed as a person who cannot rely on friends for assistance.[37] Also doesn't want to endanger.

But what about the social welfare system? Would not formal organizations offer assistance to this woman who desperately wants and needs to leave her home? According to claims—no. First of all, claims-makers argue that agency specialization, rules, and regulations often prohibit them from offering real assistance. To take only the most obvious examples, a woman might well want to leave her home at night or on the weekend when agencies are closed; she might well require immediate financial assistance even though her partner is legally responsible; she might well have many needs not fitting specialized agency mandates. But second, even if she does negotiate this bureaucratic maze, according to claims she will not be helped by the "professionals" who work in such places. According to claims, professionals treat this type of woman as the problem and they deny, discount, or ignore women's stories of brutality. On all stages of social problem construction there are many testimonials offered by women who were told by their clergy to be more tolerant, who were given anti-depressant drugs by physicians who merely treated injuries and did not even ask about their source, and who were told by counselors and psychiatrists that a woman's behavior provokes victimization. Thus, claims-makers are all but united in constructing a battered woman as a woman who will receive no adequate social services.[38]

The collective representation of the "battered woman" is of a woman who is alone in her plight. She is defined as "this outcast member of society."[39] Within this construction, such a woman *does* want to leave, yet she is unable to gather the material resources necessary to do so. Obviously, this is a public problem because social life is keeping her trapped within her continuing victimization—the problem is a woman's economic entrapment, unresponsive friends, social service providers, and the traditional organization of social services. But still, such a collective representation might not be judged sufficient to account for the unexpectable behavior of staying. After all, wife abuse can happen to *any* woman, so we certainly would expect not all such women to be economically dependent mothers with small children. Furthermore, even the most pessimistic person might find it hard to believe that all friends and social service providers would refuse to help a woman in the dire situation known as "wife abuse."

All claims constructing a battered woman as objectively trapped begin with the imputation that such a woman *does* have the motivation to leave. But other constructions portray her as a type of person who might reasonably *not* have this motivation. According to claims, a battered woman might not be economically dependent, she might not be a legal wife nor a mother, but regardless and by definition, she *is* a woman, and characteristics commonsensically and stereotypically associated with femininity describe a "battered woman," and excuse her behavior of staying even when she has an objective route to safety.

A variety of terms are used to describe the femininity of a battered woman. Often, she simply is constructed as "traditional" in her beliefs about families and women. Such a woman, for example, is constructed as one who believes that divorce is a stigma, that marriage of any quality is better than no marriage, that her children need their father. Most often described as "emotionally dependent," such a woman is constructed as one who believes she is responsible for her partner's abusive behavior. According to claims, such characteristics describe a battered woman type of person and these characteristics prevent her from defining "leaving" as the most reasonable course of action.[40]

While such associations with traditional femininity become part of the collective representation of the battered woman, they pose an implicit challenge to claims about the condition known as "wife abuse." That is, if such a woman *chooses* these beliefs, then her continued victimization is not a public problem. Claims-makers have deflected this threat by a further attribution, a battered woman type of person does not choose such traditional beliefs, she is a pure product of her environment. She is constructed, for example, as a woman who has been "*conditioned* to believe she is not complete without a man," "*conditioned* to be passive and submissive," "*conditioned* to accept dependency and to be selfless."[41] (emphases added). Since her femininity is attributed to her socialization, which was not under her control, a battered woman is constructed as a person who has been victimized by life's experiences:

> . . . the battered wife is a victim of over-socialization into a stereotypical feminine role. She has learned to be docile, submissive, humble, ingratiating, non-assertive, dependent, quiet, conforming, and selfless. Her identity is founded on being pleasing to others, but not to herself.[42]

At this point, the collective representation of the battered woman is of a stereotypical wife/mother/woman, she becomes describable as the "worst-off among all women." As such, she is not a qualitatively different type of person, she is *any* woman, she is *all* women:

> The plight of the battered woman illustrates and clarifies the issues raised by the woman's movement. For the battered woman magnifies what most women have experienced at some point in their lives.[43]

This construction of the battered woman as any woman is compatible with claims that the condition known as "wife abuse" can happen to any woman, and it is compatible with many feminist constructions label-

* ing all women as "victims of male domination." Such a construction, though, is insufficient for two reasons. First, if a battered woman is *not* a special kind of person then there is no support for claims-makers who argue that she is a "specific kind of victim," that such a woman forms a "special population," or a "specific class of citizens."[44] Second, since wife abuse is explicitly constructed as a *specific type of problem*, it follows there would be specific consequences associated with it. In brief, although a few claims-makers, particularly those identified with and writing for feminist audiences, emphasize that a battered woman is *any* woman, claims entering the public consciousness often construct her as more than a wife/mother/woman. She also is constructed as a *victim* of the specific experience known as "wife abuse."

Characteristics associated with the experience of victimization describe a battered woman and further account for her deviant behavior of staying in a relationship containing wife abuse. For example, recall that wife abuse is a label for acts experienced by victims as terrifying. Given this, it is logical that a battered woman would be constructed as a woman filled with fear who has "lived in a state of terror for so long." According to claims, the fear experienced by such a woman is more than fear for immediate safety, it is a generalized characteristic that "immobilizes them, rules their actions, their decisions, their very lives."[45] Of course, this characteristic of fear also serves to prevent a woman from leaving her home even though she might want to do so.

As constructed, a battered woman also is characterized as "emotionally confused" and this, too, is understandable. Recall that a man who abuses his wife might appear normal to outsiders, and after a violent incident he might act loving and contrite—for a while. Furthermore, recall that wife abuse is a label for events having nothing to do with a woman's characteristics or behavior. When these constructions are combined, it is only logical to construct a "battered woman" as emotionally confused. How is she to understand her experiences? According to claims, objective entrapments combine with traditional beliefs and insanity of experience to lead such a woman to "eventually lose awareness of her own needs" and to "erroneously blame herself." Such a woman is further constructed as justifiably angry, yet one who will "hide," "suppress," or "disguise" her emotions, as one who becomes "afraid to feel," as one who develops techniques to "inhibit her sense of outrage," as one who "transforms her rage and anger into depression." Such emotional confusion, furthermore, leads her to "exhibit a lack of acknowledgement that her batterer really is in control." Given this confusion, it is logical to claim that when such a woman says she loves her abuser it is because she has been "brainwashed." On all stages of social problem construction, in brief, the battered woman is constructed as a type of woman who is emotionally confused and therefore unable to define leaving as her most reasonable course of action.[46]

Still further, a "battered woman" is a woman who is routinely abused by her partner in life and how does she understand this in relation to her self? According to claims, "each beating serves to reinforce the abused woman's negative self-image." A battered woman therefore is characterized by "devastatingly low self-esteem," she "accepts the image of herself as unloveable." Such a woman, of course, might not leave because she does not believe she deserves anything better in her life.[47]

Finally, according to claims, the process of victimization might lead a battered woman type of person to develop a range of physical and psychological illnesses. In addition to injuries from the physical violence, such a person is constructed as one who is prone to develop headaches, asthma, gastrointestinal problems and chronic pain, "anxiety and depression are endemic" to such a type of woman who might "end up drinking, taking drugs prescribed by her physician for depression, abusing (her) children or attempting suicide." Clearly and most certainly, claims-makers are united in arguing that such physical and psychological illnesses are the *result* of victimization. Most claims-makers go further and construct such illnesses as *transient* reactions to abuse not existing before abuse and disappearing after abuse. But it remains that a battered woman type of person is characterized by illnesses that might well block her route to leaving a relationship containing the behaviors known as "wife abuse."[48]

In the process of accounting for the unexpectable behavior of staying in a relationship containing wife abuse, claims-makers have constructed a new collective representation—a "battered woman." The fully described ideal type would be a woman of any age, race, social class, or marital status who was in the social roles of wife and mother. Such a woman would want to leave—or would want to leave if she was not so confused as the result of her victimization—but she would be trapped within her continuing and brutal victimization by economic and emotional dependence, by friends and social service providers who refused to help, and by her traditional beliefs. Such a woman would be isolated from others, overwhelmingly fearful and emotionally confused; she would have little faith in herself and she would suffer from a range of physical and emotional illnesses that were understandable reactions to her terrible plight. This particular experience, biography, and subjectivity describes the collective representation called the "battered woman," and this collective representation excuses the unexpected behavior of staying in a relationship containing experiences known as "wife abuse."

Such a collective representation deflects challenges to the wife abuse problem posed by the behavior of women who "stay." Simultaneously, this representation furnishes a warrant for public intervention. Indeed, the representation furnishes a *mandate* for intervention since, in the final analysis, a battered woman type of person *requires* help if she is to be able to remove herself from her plight. After all, she is constructed as a person who "cannot cope with the outside world without some assistance and intervention," as "too demoralized to assert herself," as "bewildered and helpless," and as "overwhelmingly passive and unable to act on her own behalf." Such a person requires assistance since her self-image is "to the point where she has very little to work with," since she is "deficient in coping strategies," and "cognitively, emotionally, and motivationally deficient."[49] The content of the collective representation of the battered woman therefore supports the claim that this type of person is "society's problem."

As constructed, "wife abuse" is a social problem and, as constructed, the "battered woman" requires help. But what is to be done? While some claims-makers writing for feminist and academic audiences have focused attention on describing how to stop wife abuse *before* it happens, what has captured public attention is the image of the battered woman as a person needing help *now*. Public attention has focused narrowly on the immediate problem of her safety and hence, the call for "shelters for the battered woman." According to all claims-makers on every stage of social problem construction, a battered woman first and foremost needs a shelter.

Not surprisingly, claims-makers are not a united group advancing one homogeneous image of what shelters should do or how they should do it. My interest, though, is in claims about organizations that "fit" claims about problems and persons. Since the public problem called "wife abuse" is defined as behavior *not* created by women, I am not interested in shelters where a battered woman is defined as "a person who created her victimization." Furthermore, since wife abuse is defined as unstoppable violence, I am not interested in shelters seeking to save families. Shelters treating women as the problem and those focusing on repairing families now are labeled "shelters of the past," and they are explicitly contrasted with modern shelters arising from the collective representations of wife abuse and the battered woman.[50] How are such places to help this victim of wife abuse?

The collective representation of shelters

> A shelter can be a place where a woman who has lived in fear and isolation can find security and safety as well as the love and support of other women.
>
> > Jennifer Baker Fleming, *Stopping Wife Abuse*

> Most battered women, in order to leave violence, primarily need safety and support. They feel isolated and dependent and blame themselves. They need recognition that their experience is shared and that their problem is social and political, not individual.
>
> > Gail Sullivan and Jane Weiss,
> > "How We Support Battered Women"

Beginning with the public image of a battered woman as trapped because she has no place to go, it follows that shelters must offer her and her children a place to go. This is the core image of such places—they are hotels for the battered woman. More precisely, they are *emergency hotels* given claims about how a woman reaches them. She is described as the "woman who grabs her children and flees her violent husband in the middle of the night"; magazine readers are told "women often arrive at the shelter—with children—in a police car after being rescued from a beating"; social policy makers learn that most women "arrive at shelters in the middle of the night . . . frightened and injured." Furthermore, according to claims, such places might *look* like emergency hotels. A magazine article, for example, described one such place as "in shambles—bare floors, peeling wallpaper, no furniture, slabs of foam rubber propped upon telephone directories for beds," and other observers have described such places as "over-crowded," "noisy," and "disease ridden."[51]

It seems the general public has been more or less satisfied with this image of shelters as emergency hotels because this is where the vast majority of public claims stop. Granted, such places might be over-crowded—a claim supporting the call for more shelters—yet they do resolve the most immediate need of a battered woman for a place to go. Within such an image, a shelter is a black box; it is nothing but a place.

Claims-makers have focused on advocating for more shelters yet a thoughtful reader might wonder: Does an emergency hotel fulfill the needs of the battered woman who leaves her home? If such a woman was trapped only because she had no where to go, then yes, an emergency hotel would be sufficient. Thus, some claims-makers have constructed a battered woman as no longer a victim once she leaves her home: A woman's request for shelter in such claims is constructed as her "declaration of independence" from further abuse; a woman who enters a shelter is constructed as one who is "euphoric as a result of achieving liberation from years of violence and oppression."[52]

But according to other claims, when a battered woman leaves her home some of her troubles might actually worsen. She now is constructed as a person who feels guilty about leaving, a person who feels like a failure because she left; she is constructed as a person who fears for her future. It is no wonder that policy makers are told shelter clients are "women in poor condition."[53] Furthermore, given claims about the confusions of such a woman we might predict that she would check into an emergency hotel at night and then check out the next morning, still passive, confused, helpless, and dependent.

Since the battered woman has been constructed as a type of woman experiencing many troubles in addition to her lack of a place to go, it follows that, if shelters are to assist such a woman, they must offer more than emergency housing. Yet few claims made in public policy hearings or in mass media magazines go further than simply advocating the need for shelters. But the absence of claims on these public stages does not mean an end to claims-making.[54] Rather, a smaller public of shelter insiders continues to make claims. Within this set of claims written by and for academics who study shelters, persons who organize and work in such places and persons who train those who work in such places, the black box image is given specific content.

To begin, while the core image of shelters as emergency hotels fulfills the needs of a woman who needs a place to go to escape victimization, the definition of wife abuse as continuing, escalating and unstoppable behavior raises a disturbing possibility: What good is accomplished if a shelter only gives a woman a short respite from victimization? It is, bluntly stated, a troublesome image somewhat equivalent to repairing a soldier so that she can be sent back into battle only to be wounded again. Obviously, this is not the image of claims-makers, who argue that shelters should not be "simply residences, or temporary hotels along the way in women's violent lives," and that such places should not be "simply places for troubled relationships to cool off."[55] Commonsensically, given wife abuse as a label for unstoppable violence, it follows that it would be counterproductive to have an organization repeatedly used by women who kept returning to unchanged, violent relationships. As constructed, then, shelters are more than emergency housing; they *should* do something to change the situation bringing a woman to them.

Of course, organizational goals of changing situations could mean many things. Publicly, shelters are described as places helping a woman "determine her options," or helping a woman "make up her mind about the future"; policy makers are told that shelter workers ask each woman, "What do you want? What do you need?" But commonsensically, only some forms of change are compatible with the construction of the wife abuse problem. Would shelters want to help a woman become a "better wife?" No, that is not sensible given that wife abuse is violence not created by a woman's behaviors. Would a shelter want to train her in how to cope better with the violence she experiences? Of course not—as defined, a battered woman is a woman who already has such coping skills—the attitudes and behaviors which keep her trapped. Given the construction of the public problem called "wife abuse," and given the construction of the type of person called "a battered woman," only some goals for shelters are sensible. Within claims, the general goal of "effecting life change" is further operationalized; the ultimate goal is defined as the "achievement of independent living arrangements." Most simply, the goal of shelters is to keep the woman from returning to her husband.

This goal of shelter services is found in magazine articles where individual women credit such places for helping them remain away from their former abusers; this goal is implicit when claims-makers define as shelter service failures those women who use services and then return to their former partners; it is implicit when shelter rules prohibit reentry to any woman who uses services and then returns to her former home, and when shelter rules prohibit contact between shelter clients and their partners.[56] This is sensible. After all:

> . . . batterings usually escalate rather than stop when a woman returns to a battering man. Can a shelter, in good conscience, be accessory to a battering or murder by denying a woman the support she needs to get out of this situation? If many women leave a shelter to return to a battering man, it's a sure sign that the shelter has failed them in some way.[57]

As constructed, shelters have *two* service goals. They offer "a secure escape from violent men and a stepping stone to independence"; they offer "immediate protection and long-term life change."[58] As such, shelters are social service organizations and the battered woman is their client, defined as "a person requiring more than emergency housing."

So, if a battered woman is to become a successful client, she needs to become independent. What does such a woman need from a shelter? Obviously, the answer to this question depends on the image of her problems; anything encouraging a woman to stay in her relationship must be overcome. First, her need for a place to go is resolved by shelters as always open emergency hotels. But if she is to *remain* independent she will need more. At the minimum, she will need permanent housing and money to support herself and her children. But relatively few claims-makers focus on overcoming objective dependence and their logic is simple: What would be the use of helping a battered woman gain the material means to independence if her subjectivity prevented her from achieving emotional independence? Thus, shelters are constructed as "reconstitutive milieus," as places concerned primarily with "consciousness-raising." Stated most explicitly, shelter services are for the purpose of "resocializing" the battered woman. As explicitly defined, the goal of services is to produce "strong and independent women," a woman who is "emotionally independent," "emotionally detached from her husband," a woman who can "stand on her own two feet and make her own decisions," a woman who defines herself as "competent and autonomous."[59]

How should this be done? Prescriptions and proscriptions for accomplishing service objectives flow from the characteristics of the battered woman type of person. First, recall that claims about such a woman criticized social service agencies for their rules, regulations, and professionals who did not help. It follows that shelters should be different. According to claims, if a battered woman is to achieve independence, she does not need to be treated as a "subservient client," nor should she "replace control by an abusive man with control . . . by well-meaning staff"; shelters should not be places where a "passive, dependent woman looks to an expert to solve her problems."[60] Within such claims, *anything* encouraging a woman's continued dependence is labeled as counterproductive:

> If you caretake you don't give a woman what she needs. Shelters where women went back to their husbands were often shelters where they had been taken care of as opposed to being helped to develop their own survival skills.[61]

Second, it is logical that shelters should promote a political rather than a personal analysis of troubles. After all, a battered woman cannot be blamed for her troubles since, by definition, wife abuse occurs regardless of who she is or what she does. Furthermore, since no small part of her troubles stem from her tendency to blame herself, it would be illogical to continue such individual analysis. Granted, according to claims, such a woman does have much personal work to do—she needs to focus on her victimization in order to stop denying the severity of her plight; she needs to focus on her anger in order to stop denying her emotional outrage. But since her troubles are all situationally imposed rather than character defects, most claims-makers deny the relevance of psychological therapy. While this might be a point where shelter insiders depart from the general public, which holds great faith in the power of therapy and counseling, shelter insiders often prohibit therapy, for it implies that a woman is sick, reinforces her self-blame, and promotes dependence on a therapist. Within such claims, only "feminist therapy" sometimes is promoted with the argument that this specific form of therapy increases the woman's feeling of being in control of her life.[62]

Beginning with the contents of the collective representation of the battered woman type of person, several aspects of shelter organization follow. Such places should be emergency hotels, but they also should be social services, but then again, they should not be social services in the traditional sense. What is deemed good for the battered woman is an organization offering services without authority structures, rules, professionals, or individual treatment.[63]

While this might seem to leave few resources, there is a logical relationship between claims about what shelters should do and the collective representation of the battered woman. Recall that this type of person's troubles are all created by the environment; they are the consequences of being a woman in sexist society, of being socialized into stereotypical feminine attitudes and behaviors, of being oppressed, victimized, dependent, and trapped. Within such a purely environmental theory of causation, it is logical to promote a purely environmental theory of change. As constructed, shelters offer no more and no less than an oppositional environment to the one creating the battered woman type of person. Such places, according to constructions, should offer *(a)* an environment *empowering* the woman whose troubles stem from her powerlessness, *(b)* an environment encouraging *independence* for this woman who has known only dependence, *(c)* an environment *supporting* this woman who has been isolated and ignored, and *(d)* an environment encouraging *high self-esteem* for this woman who always has blamed herself. According to claims, shelters offer

> . . . a social context in which alternative ideologies and behaviors are necessary and workable; a milieu in which women see other women acting authoritatively, behaving independently in situations which require independent decision-making.[64]

Two key ideas, community and individual responsibility, define the philosophical foundations of shelters. First, according to constructions, shelters offer *communal living*, and this community of women is defined as the single most important ingredient of shelter service success."[65]

Claims-makers argue that this community of women reduces the isolation a battered woman has experienced, and that close living with other women encourages women to share their experiences. According to claims, such "sharing of commonalities and differences with others helps offset their previous deprivation." Furthermore, according to claims, the constant talk among women living together encourages them to "express their anger, reject responsibility for violence and overcome feelings of guilt and inadequacy." Thus, shelters contain peer support among women which replaces traditional psychotherapy. This substitution is made logical by claims that each client will discover "other women have had the same experiences and felt basically the same emotions" and "most women have skills necessary to be supportive listeners."[66] In brief, shelters accomplish their service goals primarily by allowing the battered woman to live with other such women:

> When a woman first comes in contact with a shelter group, the most refreshing and powerful aspect of her encounter is that her experience is *validated*. . . . Not only does she feel a tremendous sense of relief, but of empowerment.[67]

These claims, of course, modify the image of shelters as emergency hotels. Unlike hotels where guests occupy private rooms and most often remain strangers to one another, a shelter is more like a sorority house where members share living space and where satisfying face-to-face interaction is possible because of shared experiences. By definition, women in shelters share the characteristics associated with their membership in the social collectivity called the "battered woman."

But this image is insufficient. A shelter is not a long slumber party because there is much to be done if a woman is to remain independent. How is this work accomplished? According to claims, shelters promote individual responsibility; self-help is labeled as the "fundamental principle of shelter organization."[68] According to claims, since a battered woman type of person is immobilized because she feels worthless and incompetent, it follows she needs responsibilities and the opportunity to take charge of her life. So, within shelters, each woman is to be responsible for herself and her children, each shares responsibility for cleaning communal living areas, and generally running the place. Each of these activities is constructed as positive and empowering. Indeed, claims-makers argue that mundane responsibilities such as communal meal preparation and housekeeping are especially important because they are areas where "traditional women can display their competence to others and thus increase their self-esteem."[69] Such individual and communal responsibilities, in other words, are constructed as the way to achieve service goals since "when residents take initiative . . . they begin to develop a sense of capability and confidence that is one of the most valuable resources a refuge can impart."[70]

Within such an image, there is little need for organizational employees. Indeed, the very idea of workers—persons formally in charge—poses problems within claims promoting independence *via* self-determination and self-help. Thus, shelter workers can be defined as a "threat to self-help." Not surprisingly, therefore, there are few claims about workers and most of these are in the form of warnings: Workers must not be professionals; they must not think of themselves as different from their clients; they must not tell clients what to do; they must not allow clients to "transfer dependence." Within such constructions, it is not clear what workers *should* do. A few claims do promote workers as "role models" demonstrating that "women can act independently and authoritatively," but this is countered by other claims: workers should learn as much from clients as clients learn from workers and both groups should share the same organizational status of "women helping women." Likewise, although some constructions are of workers as advocates helping clients gather necessary financial and legal resources for independence, others maintain this threatens the general sanctions against "doing for" women.[71]

In the final analysis, there are few constructions of shelter workers, or these persons are constructed merely as other women—the stable members of the shelter community. Within such images, the job of workers is simply "being there."

In summary, the shelter goal of transforming a battered woman type of person into the anthetical type of a "strong woman" is constructed as accomplished through the environment. Within this representation, shelter clients themselves establish this environment; they accomplish everything themselves, and through this experience they become capable and strong women:

The women living in the refuge organize and run the day-to-day affairs of the house. . . . Decisions about the general operation of the refuge . . . are made on a collective basis. . . . Through the process of living in a refuge and beginning to assume more responsibility for their lives and taking part in running the refuge, most women quickly regain the self-confidence and self-esteem they may have lost.[72]

This is the process of transforming a battered woman into a strong woman. Claims-makers are very optimistic about the power of this model. They claim this environment will "quickly reverse the deficits" a battered woman has accumulated; they claim when such a woman enters such a place she will "flower"; they claim this environment will produce a woman who "can no longer be battered."[73]

Taken together, these claims construct the collective representation of shelters for the battered woman type of person. So it seems the public image of such places is confirmed by shelter observers, workers, and organizers. That is, in the composite image there are no "programs," "therapy," "rules," "professionals," or "organizational representatives." The image of shelters is of a large woman-only extended family, a family freely chosen by its members, a family whose composition continually changes with the arrival and departure of women, a family where each member shares the characteristics of the "battered woman" and a family engaged in mutual sharing and support. Within such an image a shelter *is* merely a place.

Clearly, shelters are specifically for the battered woman. They offer what this type of person needs and, critically, the probable success of this type of organization would depend on clients who were this type of person. For example, a critical reader might challenge the assumption that clients would enjoy their shelter stays. Would not women object to living in shelters described in terms such as dismal, overcrowded, and disease ridden? According to claims, this is not a problem. Since each client is a battered woman escaping the devastation of wife abuse, it follows that "surroundings do not matter when you're running for your life." Thus, magazine readers are told that, although many clients come from comfortable homes and end up sleeping on mattresses on the floor, they are simply grateful for the chance to be free. Indeed, since it encourages clients to overcome their isolation, claims-makers even argue that overcrowding is *beneficial*.[74]

A critical reader might also wonder about the probability of establishing a "therapeutic" community of women within such places. After all, since a battered woman can be a woman of any race, age, or social class, married or single, a college graduate or illiterate, we would expect that at any one time shelter clients would be a heterogeneous group. Yet the battered woman collective representation meets this challenge. A battered woman type of person, by definition, would be a good commune member. Defined in terms of her passivity, low self-esteem, other-directedness, fear, confusion and helplessness, we would not expect her to be a disruptive member of the shelter commune. Indeed, we would anticipate that such a woman would be a good commune member since she would be highly attuned to others and try to please them. Furthermore, while women in shelters might be very dissimilar to one another in terms of personal characteristics, claims-makers focus on what they share—the status of a battered woman.[75] Clearly, shelters are for this type of woman. They are specifically organized for her, they depend on her to want and need what the organization offers, they depend on her to become a good member of the shelter community of women.

Summary

♦ Dynamic nominalism remains an intriguing doctrine, arguing that numerous kinds of human beings and human acts come into being hand in hand with our invention of the categories labeling them.

Ian Hacking, "Making Up People"

It is common for claims-makers to argue that wife abuse always has existed and was simply "invisible" prior to the 1970s when claims-makers brought this to public attention. Within the social construction approach to public problems we rather would say that prior to the 1970s, wife abuse did not exist. Most certainly, some husbands always have victimized their wives—the historical record is clear on that—but assault could not be an instance of "wife abuse" until the label was available. The label is that of a collective representation. Likewise, although the historical record shows that some women always have been victimized by their husbands, these women could not be instances of the "battered woman" until this label and categorization were constructed. In this view, social problems claims-makers *created* the problem called "wife abuse," they *created* the type of person called a "battered woman." Just as certainly, these representations created the need for a specific type of social service: A service for this particular type of person who experiences this particular type of problem. Hence, wife abuse, the battered woman, and shelters are an internally logical package of social problem constructions.

This is the first type of social problems work, the human activity of constructing some conditions as "problems," the activity of constructing some types of persons as "victims." Out of the broad, objective reality of *all* violence toward women, wife abuse is about violence that is severe, frequent, unstoppable, and multiply-consequential; it is about violence in which men are offenders and women are victims. Likewise, out of the broad, objective reality of *all* women experiencing victimization, the battered woman has been constructed as a woman with a particular set of experiences, a particular biography, a particular constellation of personal characteristics, subjectivities, and motivations. Thus, when I argue that wife abuse and the battered woman are socially constructed, this is what I mean: Not all violence is that of wife abuse, not all victimized women are instances of the battered woman. Only some forms of violence, only some victimized women have been socially constituted as objects for public attention.

Since wife abuse and the battered woman explicitly and implicitly distinguish among types of violence and types of women, a second kind of social problems work is necessary. This is the work of *reproducing* these categories, the work of *applying* these categories to social life. Wife abuse and the battered woman are socially reproduced each time a social member evaluates a specific, unique practical experience as that of "wife abuse," and each time a social member evaluates a specific, unique, individual woman as a "battered woman." This is a social process, the process of distinguishing between violence that is the violence of wife abuse and the violence *not* that of wife abuse; it is the process of deciding which women experiencing violence belong in the category battered woman and which victimized women do *not*. This second type of social problems work is ongoing; it is the work of evaluating practical experience on a case by case basis; the work of deciding when social categories should be applied to particular experiences and to particular people. I turn now to this work of evaluating practical experience.

Chapter Two

Schemes of Interpretation and Practical Experience

An answer is only seen to be the right one if it sustains the institutional thinking that is already in the minds of individuals as they try to decide.

Mary Douglas, *How Institutions Think*

So far, I have been arguing that wife abuse and the battered woman are Durkheimian collective representations; they are publicly standardized images of conditions and types of people. As such, they also are Schutzian schemes of interpretation, or frameworks available to organize and make sense of social experience. Yet as Gale Miller and James Holstein note, any particular scheme of interpretation is only a "candidate structure," only one of countless ways to categorize reality. Given there are innumerable ways to categorize any unique experience, interpretive work is necessary on a case by case basis.[1]

This is a second type of social problems work. Certainly, claims about wife abuse and the battered woman yielded new collective representations, but these representations continue to exist only as long as social members use them as interpretive devices. That is, the social problem called "wife abuse" continues to exist only as long as social members use that label to categorize particular experiences, the "battered woman" continues to exist only as long as individual women are incorporated into that category. In this chapter I will examine this social problems work of evaluating practical experience and particular people. This discussion has two interrelated parts. First, to label a practical experience as one of "wife abuse" and to label an individual woman as "a battered woman" is to take a particular *moral* stance toward these behaviors and persons. My first task is to examine these issues of morality underlying categorization. Second, there is the issue of linking these interpretive structures to practical experience: What must be subjectively apprehended about particular events and people in order to assign them to the wife abuse and the battered woman categories?

Social problems and moral stances

> . . . you might keep in mind that the Government role here, has, by definition, to be limited. Government can't necessarily take on the burden of making better or happier people. . . . Government can hardly structure happiness and government can hardly structure sensitivity or caring or love, you know.
>
> James H. Scheuer, "Comment"[2]

To label a condition as a social problem is to take a moral stand: The condition is intolerable and it is the public's responsibility to do something about it. Likewise, to claim a woman deserves public sympathy is to take a moral stand toward her. To be viable, social problems claims of any type must convince the public that such moral stances and public interventions are justified. While this always is a complicated matter, in the case of wife abuse it is further complicated by the fact that accepting this as a social problem is to advocate intervention into private life—something Americans are prone to dislike. Therefore, to be a social problem, wife abuse must be judged so morally intolerable as to override usual preferences for family privacy. Thus, the question: What are the moral limits to the wife abuse problem as constructed?

I first became fascinated with this question of moral limits when I started teaching a course in family violence. On the first day of class, I always ask students to write specific questions they would like answered and invariably they want me to tell them what family violence *is*. Typical questions they ask about the boundaries of wife abuse illustrate aspects of the American interpretive scheme for the moral evaluation of violence; they implicitly make visible what is and what is not collectively defined as morally intolerable.

One of the most common questions I have heard is in the form, "I want to know how far you can go before an act becomes violent," or "I'm wondering where the line is drawn between normal violence and wife abuse." For these to be heard as *sensible* questions, there must be an assumption that "wife abuse" differs from "normal violence." For these to be heard as *relevant* questions, there must be an assumption that the category "normal violence" is morally tolerable and therefore not a public problem.

These types of questions illustrate a key element in American beliefs—not all violence is a moral problem. Indeed, it seems within the conventional interpretive scheme for the moral evaluation of violence that not all violence is even labeled as "violence." Americans tend not to use the term, violence, behaviorally; we tend to reserve it for incidents where we disapprove of the use of force. Hence, few Americans label parental spanking of their children as "violence." This differentiation between normal and not normal violence is visible when social service providers reserve the term, "marital violence," for events they explicitly define as "more than the normal rough and tumble of marriage"; such differentiations also are visible when claims-makers empirically distinguish between "normal" and "abusive" violence and when they are clear that wife abuse is a label for *not normal* violence.[3]

What, then, distinguishes culturally tolerated, normal violence from the not tolerated, not normal violence condemned in the wife abuse categorization system? While many studies have examined dimensions distinguishing "child abuse" from "parental punishment," little attention has been given to this issue for wife abuse.[4] I can only piece together some glimpses of underlying dimensions.

Most clearly, a major dimension of normality or non-normality is the *extremity* of behavior. In commonsense reasoning, a slap is more normal than a punch and this is more normal than stabbing with a knife. Such reasoning promotes the evaluation of extreme sounding forms of behavior as "not normal," and this, in turn, is supported by probability reasoning: What is the likelihood that injury will result from this form of violence? This folk reasoning also is apparent when claims-makers define as "abuse" those acts *likely to yield injury* to victims.[5]

Second, although Americans tend to use probability reasoning to associate severity of violence with probable consequences, the cultural interpretive scheme also evaluates *actual injury*—regardless of how it was produced. In some ways, what is and what is not evaluated as normal or not normal violence can only be known in retrospect when the event is concluded and the consequences are known. In law, for example, an "attempt to do harm" receives less sanction than "doing harm"; to cause injury is not as bad as to cause serious injury, and this is not as bad as to cause permanent injury, and so on.[6] Thus, the legal code reflects the general cultural interpretation: the more violence is consequential, the more it is morally intolerable.

Third, Americans evaluate the "normality" of violence by judging the *intent* of the person using it. Student questions such as: "How can you tell if it's violence or just anger," or "How do you classify differences between acts occurring out of anger and acts with intent to do harm," illustrate the belief that intentionality of violence is both knowable and important. This interpretive scheme also is enshrined in law since to be sanctioned for the use of violence an offender must intend to do harm—accidents are unfortunate but morally tolerable.[7]

Finally, the cultural interpretive scheme for the moral evaluation of violence judges the *worthiness of reasons for its use*. Student questions such as, "Does it count if a wife hits her husband after he attacked her," or "Does it count as wife abuse if the husband is very drunk," assume there are good reasons for violence, or at least reasons neutralizing its illegitimacy. The use of this interpretive scheme is visible in research findings indicating that men and women alike tend to tolerate or are willing to forgive violence when the offender is judged to be drunk, overwrought, or frustrated; it is enshrined in law where duress and mental disease neutralize wrongdoing. Violence likewise is not morally condemned when it is judged a reasonable response to victim behavior. These cultural evaluations, too, are visible in the legal code where self-defense, provocation, and combat by agreement each neutralize the illegitimacy of a violent act.[8]

Since violence associated with wife abuse is extreme *and* consequential *and* intended *and* done for no "good reason," this social problem categorization system does not challenge these dimensions of the American interpretive scheme for the moral evaluation of violence. Indeed, claims-makers explicitly have argued that an incident of wife abuse should be judged as is any other incident of violence. Their complaint is that wife abuse has been subjected to different moral criteria allowing men to engage in any brutality without censure. As a consequence, to evaluate a particular incident as one of wife abuse is not necessarily to step outside the general cultural interpretation system for the moral evaluation of violence. The public is asked to condemn as wife abuse only those incidents of violence that are obviously outside moral boundaries.[9]

In constructing wife abuse as a public problem, claims-makers asked the public to morally condemn some types of violence. They also argued that women experiencing this violence should receive public sympathy and we can look at the underlying moral dimension of this claim.

According to Candace Clark, sympathy is a social commodity and as such there are cultural conventions surrounding it. According to her, in order to have a claim to sympathy, a person must be judged as being in a "dire situation," as "not complicit" in creating their problems, and as "morally worthy."[10] If a battered woman is to be accorded sympathy *because* she is a "battered woman," then either this type of person must be constructed as one who deserves sympathy as determined by cultural evaluations of sympathy worthiness, or the rules of sympathy must be changed for her.

Obviously, a battered woman is in a dire situation—that is contained within the collective representation of wife abuse. But is she complicit in creating her troubles? By definition, of course, she does nothing to provoke her victimization, but, since she remains in her situation, she might still be evaluated as complicit. The persistence of the question, why does she stay, makes visible the American interpretive structure of individualism and its biases toward making sense of all behaviors in terms of individual choice and defining all remedial action as individual responsibility.[11] Within this general scheme, if a battered woman chooses to remain for any reason then, bluntly stated, it is her choice and she does not deserve sympathy. But certainly, this does not describe this type of woman. Does she stay because she does not mind her abuse? Certainly not. Does she stay because she self-consciously and freely chooses to do so? Definitely not. As constructed, the battered woman type of person is worthy of sympathy because she is in a dire situation, and because she is not complicit in creating her own troubles.

But is she morally worthy? The collective representation does not contain anything leading us to label a battered woman as morally unworthy. Indeed, as constructed, this type of person is trapped within her victimization precisely because she acts in conventionally approved ways—she is a good woman, a good wife and a good mother. Furthermore, the collectivity reformulates many characteristics that typically are morally contaminating. For example, a social actor who is an alcoholic or a drug user does not have an indisputable claim to sympathy. Likewise, the general scheme of individualism leads the public to typically not feel sympathy for persons who do not help themselves. Yet claims construct such possible characteristics of the battered woman as mere consequences of her victimization. Such a woman, for example, is constructed as one who might appear lazy or apathetic but only because she is "immobilized by her trauma," "depressed over her plight," or "paralyzed by her fear." Claims further construct her as a woman who might turn to drugs or alcohol as a reaction to her plight.[12] Since each such morally contaminating characteristic is constructed as a reaction to victimization, they support rather than threaten the evaluation of a "battered woman" as a morally deserving person.

In brief, for the public to offer a woman sympathy, they must label her as a person in dire need, as one who is not complicit in her victimization and as morally deserving. Since the collective representation of the battered woman is of a woman meeting all these tests for sympathy worthiness, this conventional interpretive scheme is not challenged. There are no claims that sympathy should be given to a woman who "deserves" or "likes" to be hit, and no claims that a "truly lazy" or a "truly alcoholic" woman should be given sympathy. But a battered woman type of person is not such a morally contaminated actor. She *is* deserving of public sympathy.[13]

In summary, there is a necessary underlying logic to viable social problems claims in modern day America. Since Americans tend to define as social problems only those conditions defined as morally intolerable, since we tend to withhold sympathy from all but pure victims in desperate situations, viable claims will construct problems and people in ways compatible with these underlying interpretive structures. The wife abuse categorization system therefore asks for the moral condemnation of violence that is intolerable as judged within the general interpretive scheme for the moral evaluation of violence; the battered woman categorization system asks that sympathy be offered to women who should receive sympathy as evaluated within the general interpretive scheme for the moral evaluation of people. Such implicit evaluations are made each time social actors decide whether or not a given experience is one of "wife abuse," whether or not a given woman is a "battered woman." Yet this begs the question: How are evaluations actually accomplished?

Interpretive schemes and practical experience

> . . . it is easy to conceive of situations in which we have an obviously battered woman, I mean they may be unconscious on the living room floor, and a perpetrator with cloven hooves and a pitchfork standing over her. . . . But frequently police encounter a far different picture . . . in which they may get very different reports of what happened, and in which it may take some time to figure out what's going on.
>
> Carol Corrigan, "Testimony"

Any scheme of interpretation is only a candidate structure, only one possible way to make sense of practical experience. To grant a social problem label is to take a moral stance, yet this relies on interpretive work.

Wife abuse and the battered woman collective representations are examples of what Alfred Schutz calls "scientific constructs." Such constructs are *abstract* because they do not concern individuals with unique characteristics; they are *limited* because they contain only those characteristics deemed pertaining to the issue at hand; they are *simplified* because they bracket the idiosyncratic meanings and difficulties of practical actors in daily life.[14] Scientific constructs, in other words, bracket the uniqueness, ambiguity, and heterogeneity of practical experience, which is not confined to "within these constructions." Hence, my questions: What must be subjectively apprehended in order to define a unique experience as one of wife abuse? What must be subjectively apprehended in order to define a particular woman as a battered woman?

First and most obviously, wife abuse must be differentiated from the larger category of "family troubles." Alcoholism, mental illness, drug addiction, problems with slovenly, untruthful or untrustable family members, poverty, and homelessness are each troubles, but they are not the particular troubles called "wife abuse." To label a particular trouble as one of wife abuse, an evaluator must distinguish among different types of troubles, a difficult task, of course, because family troubles most often occur in complex constellations.

As constructed, wife abuse is about violence. In particular, it is about the "not normal" violence done by men on women, with "not normal" being those incidents where violence sounds severe, where there are injuries, where there is intent to do harm, and where there is no justification. So, to be labeled as an incident of "wife abuse," the *violence* must be evaluated.

While illustrative cases used by claims-makers typically meet *all* criteria for wife abuse, practical experience is heterogeneous. First, commonsense notions of the relationship between severity of violence and consequences, in practice, do not always pertain. A slap might sound normal, but what if a *particular* slap knocks the victim to the floor? Is that particular slap still normal?[15] Second, while wife abuse is about recurring violence, what does this mean? The collective representation gives an image of violence occurring frequently, but what if in a *particular* relationship the violence occurs regularly once every two years? Is that enough to evaluate it as patterned and therefore wife abuse? Third, wife abuse is violence done with the intent of doing harm, but intent is knowable only to the person using violence and even here there are many practical possibilities. What if a *particular* man did intend to throw something but did not intend for the object to actually hit his wife? How do we judge intent? What if a *particular* man did intend to slap his wife but did not intend for her to suffer injury? How is his intent judged? Fourth, wife abuse is about violence done for no·good reason. Yet commonsensically, what does and what does not constitute a "good reason" varies in relation to the severity of the act and the consequences. Is it morally tolerable, for example, for a man to slap his wife when he learns she has just gambled away his entire life savings? Obviously, illustrations constructing wife abuse are those of non-justifiable violence—a woman brutally beaten because she did not cook a meal fast enough—but in real life the severity of the violence and its consequences vary as do the reasons given for the violence. Fifth, the collective representation of wife abuse contains many characteristics that can be *independent* in practical experience: What if in a particular situation the violence is severe but not particularly frequent or consequential? What if it is frequent but never severe?

Finally but critically, the interpretive scheme for evaluating violence is like any other interpretive device in that the recipes for evaluation are open-ended. The implicit categorization rules are endless since each situation will have its own unique elements deemed possibly pertaining. What if a woman is a healthy twenty-three-year-old and her partner is a frail seventy-year-old? What if she is blind? What if she is pregnant? There is no end to specific characteristics that might pertain to neutralize—or emphasize—the moral intolerability of a given experience. Interpretive schemes are applied situationally and in the final evaluation, "normality" will be a composite evaluation assessing severity *and* frequency *and* consequences *and* intent *and* justifications and *whatever else is deemed relevant for that particular situation.* The typical, in other words, is evaluated only within the unique, the atypical, and the particular.[16]

In bracketing the gray areas of experience, the wife abuse collective representation was formed with precisely and primarily those cases where there would be considerable agreement about moral evaluations while in practical experience there is heterogeneity and unclarity. Critically, this complexity in evaluating individual experience is not circumvented by "professional training," since social service providers use these same general evaluative criteria.[17] In general, we might predict that the collective representation of wife abuse would be subjectively apprehended most often when violence was clearly and most assuredly "not normal." As characteristics of particular events fade into a category of "maybe normal violence," there would be less and less agreement about the applicability of assigning the experience to this category.

In brief, to define a specific event as one of wife abuse requires an evaluation of the violence. But this is not enough. The designation of wife abuse is also an automatic evaluation of the relationship within which it occurs. That is, an instance of wife abuse must occur within a relationship categorized as "abusive." No doubt there are many actual relationships where evaluators would see nothing but abuse—those where the woman always was treated as a mere object to be controlled. But this does not encompass all practical experience. Indeed, claimsmakers who find abusive relationships often include periods of relative calm acknowledge that such relationships are more than abuse. Of course, within the wife abuse collective representation, these periods of calm are constructed as only temporary respites from violence, but it remains this construction relies on the prediction that *abuse will recur*, a prediction whose truth in practical experience is known only in retrospect.

Finally and simply, to evaluate a particular incident as one of wife abuse and to evaluate a particular relationship as abusive is to assign victim and offender labels—he becomes known as an "abusive man" and she becomes known as a "battered woman." This, too, is difficult given that the collective representations are uni-dimensional while practical experience offers relatively few classic exemplars of pure "types of people."

In summary, to evaluate a specific event as one of wife abuse requires evaluating behavior, relationships, and people. I have three major points about the complexities of making these evaluations. The first is that while the battered woman type of person has been constructed as a woman who is uniquely hesitant to label her experiences as those of "wife abuse," such confusions are general because they are built into the interpretive scheme for the moral evaluation of violence; such evaluations are made more difficult by the collective representation linking such violence with particular kinds of relationships and to particular kinds of people. So, I am arguing that it is not just victims who tend to withhold the label of "wife abuse" until violence is clearly extreme, frequent, and consequential.

But it is true that the closer the evaluator is to the actual experience, relationship, and person, the more difficult it will be to evaluate an incident as one of wife abuse and this is my second point: It is not surprising that a victimized woman often sees violence as only one aspect of her relationship—*it is*. And, it is not surprising that a victimized woman might see her partner as more than a brute and describe him in positive terms—few persons *are* recognizable simply as one-dimensional brutes. But of course, when evaluators know a woman only as she is a victim then such evaluations are simply nonsense. It is, after all, difficult to comprehend a battered woman having *any* satisfactions since she is known only as she is a "battered woman"; it does not matter that "apart from the violence" she might find happiness since the collective representation does not contain aspects of her life "apart from the violence";

it does not matter that she finds positive characteristics in her partner since within the representation all that matters is that he is a brute.[18] So, this is my second point: Scientific constructs of any type bracket individual meaning; they are partial, abstract, and simplified. The closer an evaluator is to the practical experience, and the more that is known about individual actors, the more difficult it will be to see the experience as an obvious example of the collective representation.

My third point is about the dual use of collective representations as images to convince the public that a social problem is at hand and as interpretive devices to make sense of practical experience. To be viable for social problem construction, claims bracket the messiness of social life; they offer clear and vivid images of the problem at hand. Yet what is neatly bracketed in collective representations is not so neatly bracketed in lived realities. Diagnosing a specific incident as one of "wife abuse" is not like diagnosing tooth decay. There is no x-ray; there is professional or lay agreement only at the extreme; judgments always are situated and multidimensional. So true, the label "wife abuse" has entered public consciousness, but the practical question of my students remains: How do we know wife abuse when we see it? The collective representation does not furnish answers; it supplies only vague interpretive schemes awaiting to be applied within the heterogeneity, complexity, and confusion of daily life. This must be on-going social problems work, the activity of using collective representations as interpretive devices to make sense of practical experience.

In a variation on the same theme, we can ask about evaluating particular women. How do we recognize a "battered woman" when we see her? By definition, a battered woman is one who has experienced wife abuse so therefore it should follow that labeling practical experience as wife abuse would automatically label the woman as a "battered woman." But the logic of these collective representations is more complex because an incident cannot be one of wife abuse unless the woman is a battered woman, a woman who does not cause her abuse, who does not like her abuse, and a woman who remains within her abuse because she is unable to leave. So, the violence cannot be evaluated without simultaneously evaluating the victim; evaluations of conditions and persons are inextricably linked.

In the case of evaluating wife abuse and the battered woman, there are complexities arising from the constructions of these representations. This behavior happens behind closed doors so outside evaluators might well not have the information necessary to make the complicated inter-pretations. Indeed, since an abusive man and an abusive relationship are constructed as people and events often appearing normal to outsiders, it is likely information available to outsiders will be deceiving when wife abuse actually is happening. This leaves us with testimonies of involved persons, but the constructions of both victim and offender leads to the prediction that neither party is prone to label themselves or their experi-ences in terms of these representations. After all, an abusive man is con-structed as one who denies his wrongdoing and a battered woman is constructed as a woman who is prone to denial and emotional confusion. Given this, how do we know when an individual woman is an instance of the battered woman?

This identification problem has not gone unnoticed by claims-mak-ers. There have been many constructions of "what to look for" in iden-tifying the battered woman; claims-makers have produced checklists, inventories, and screening devices giving rules for "how to recognize a battered woman." For example, one such construction tells evaluators to consider diagnosing a woman as a battered woman if she is unwilling to discuss her injuries, if she is fearful in emotional expression, if she is self-deprecating and passive; another advises that the label should be considered when a woman is not active in social life, when she goes no where without her partner, when she appears nervous and seldom has cash.[19] Of all the lists of things to look for in evaluating a particular woman, the most popular and practically important is the list devised by Lenore Walker:

COMMON CHARACTERISTICS OF BATTERED WOMEN:
. . . Has low self-esteem, believes all the myths about battering rela-tionships; is a traditionalist about the home, strongly believes in family unity and the prescribed feminine sex-role stereotype; accepts responsibility for the batterer's actions; suffers from guilt, yet denies the terror and anger she feels; presents a passive face to the world but has the strength to manipulate her environment enough to prevent further violence and being killed; has severe stress reactions, with psychophysiological complaints; uses sex as a

way to establish intimacy; believes that no one will be able to help her resolve her predicament except herself.[20]

Although different constructions have been offered for identifying the battered woman in practical experience, each list shares three characteristics. First, each contains a *constellation* of characteristics. It is not enough for a given woman to be beaten, or to have one characteristic of the battered woman. A battered woman is a type of person; it is the gestalt that matters. Second, the collective representation of the battered woman is the *organizing* device for these lists. On these lists—and only on these lists—are characteristics associated with the battered woman type of person. Third, evaluators must use *commonsense interpretive techniques* to evaluate individual women. Since a woman experiencing wife abuse cannot be trusted to incorporate herself into the category, battered woman, evaluators must look for signs of her entrapment, her victimization and her emotional confusion. Stated otherwise, a battered woman can be evaluated only through the documentary method of interpretation. An evaluator must begin with knowledge of the battered woman type of person, and the characteristics of an individual woman must be compared with the collective representation. When a gestalt seemingly fits the collective representation, then a given woman is a battered woman; if the gestalt does not fit then she is not.[21] Clearly, this work of evaluating individuals is the social problems work of reproducing this image: Only those women conforming to the preexisting image are allowed into the collectivity, others are denied entry and hence, the social collectivity is reproduced.

Summary

> To recognize a class of things is to polarize and to exclude. It involves drawing boundaries, a very different activity from grading.
>
> Mary Douglas, *How Institutions Think*

Social problem collective representations are constructed by claimsmakers seeking to convince the public that a problem is at hand and that something must be done. It is to be expected that viable claims will be those constructing extreme images of conditions that are clearly intolerable, and that viable claims will be those constructing images of victims as "pure." In the case of wife abuse, claims-makers were required to circumvent long held public assumptions that violence toward women was not severe nor consequential, and that women somehow "deserved" to be hit. Changing such traditional beliefs, of course, required extreme images of wife abuse and the battered woman.

Thus, while the shape of claims is an outcome of the American public's tendency to withhold sympathy from all but pure victims and to label as social problems only extremely troublesome conditions, it remains that the collective representations of wife abuse and the battered woman commonsensically fit only a small proportion of real life experience and only a small proportion of victimized women. To be perfectly clear, I am certainly *not* arguing that the type of violence known as "wife abuse" rarely occurs, nor am I arguing that few women are seeable as instances of the battered woman type of person. Such violence and such women are all too commonly found in modern day America. My argument here is more subtle: While there are innumerable instances of violence classifiable as that of "wife abuse," such violence is only the tip of the iceberg of violence and family troubles; while there are innumerable victimized women classifiable as instances of the battered woman, there are an untold number of victimized women who do not clearly conform to such expectations.

Hence, there is the social problems work of the case by case classification of unique experience and people. Here I have used a wide lens to examine the general parameters of this work. To incorporate particular events and particular persons into the categories of wife abuse and the battered woman is to take a moral stance toward them; it is to accomplish complex, multidimensional, and situated decision-making; it is to transform the heterogeneity of lived realities into the homogeneity of social types. Regardless of complexities, a particular event becomes one of "wife abuse" or it does not; a particular woman becomes an instance of the "battered woman" or she does not.

This social problems work is accomplished whenever any practical actor evaluates a particular event and a particular person and decides whether or not incorporation into the collective representation is appropriate. Yet I want to turn now to a critical site for this work, a social service agency. Within places such as shelters for the battered woman heterogeneous and ambiguous personal troubles meet the homogeneous and clear images of collective representations; within such places collective representations of what should be done meet the practicalities of what can be done; within such places varying evaluations of the definitions and meanings of practical experience directly confront each other; within such places individual social members are officially constituted as members of a social collectivity such as battered woman.

The first type of social problems work within such places is the work of translating collective images into concrete organizational form, rules, and procedures. This work is critical because it institutionalizes collective representations—any given organizational framework will allow and encourage some types of practical action and discourage or prevent others. So, I turn now to South Coast, a place organized specifically and explicitly for the "battered woman."

Chapter Three

Collective Representations and the Formal Organization of Shelter Work

After having reviewed all the supposed options open to battered women, I have reached the conclusion that the creation of shelters designed specifically for battered women is the only direct, immediate, and satisfactory solution to the problem of wife abuse.

Del Martin, *Battered Wives*

I want to focus specifically on formal social problems work, the work accomplished in social service agencies designed to do something about morally intolerable conditions. This adds considerable complexity. While informal evaluations of problems and persons must be accomplished within the ambiguities and complexities of lived reality, formal social problems work *also* occurs within organizations. Thus, evaluators are agency representatives who work within specific organizational contexts which bring various constellations of possibilities and constraints. So, to understand formal social problems work I must examine the surrounding organizational characteristics, in this case, the characteristics of a shelter for the battered woman.[1]

Since each organization is unique, I will narrow my focus to one shelter I call "South Coast." I hope to accomplish two objectives in describing this organization. First, I want to illustrate a type of social problems work, the work of translating collective images into concrete organizational form within practical constraints. Second and most important, this discussion sets the organizational stage for examining the work of front-line social service providers who routinely accomplish the

activities of recognizing, identifying, and responding to the social problem called "wife abuse." At South Coast, this work was accomplished
within a particular ideological and organizational background of high
ideals, but it was work accomplished within myriad limitations.

Collective representations and the organization of South Coast

> When I first saw the LEAA proposal, I saw "family, family,
> family." I feel that this was to get funding. . . . My philosophy is
> the feminist core is central to this program. It's a woman's
> issue. . . . Try to see this as a woman's issue with the goal to
> give the woman some sense of self-esteem and world-readiness.
> See that they can make it on their own.
> Family Violence Program Administrator

In the fall of 1976, a group of women representing a local university
and the local Commission on Women sponsored a conference on the
battered woman where Del Martin, a well-known claims-maker in the
battered women's movement, was the keynote speaker. At the end of this
conference, these women established a special task force, and during the
next two years they gathered data to justify the need for a shelter. Ulti-
mately, they secured funding from the county and from the Comprehensive Employment and Training Act (CETA).[2] During the first year,
South Coast was under the umbrella of the local Community Action
Commission. During the next three years, when I collected my data, it
retained its county and CETA funding, but was administered by the
"Family Violence Program" (FVP), which was funded primarily by the
Law Enforcement Assistance Administration (LEAA). I shall return to
the relationship between South Coast and its umbrella organization but
for now there is one important point. Unlike some shelters where funding is through government offices such as "mental health," "alcoholism," or "welfare," South Coast received general funds carrying only
two stipulations: Services were to be offered only to women who resided
in the county, and although the battered woman was defined as the priority client, South Coast was to serve *any* woman in need of temporary
housing (women-in-transition) if space was available.[3]

South Coast was located on the outskirts of a medium-sized west coast city. The facility was rented from the county for a token one dollar a year rent. It was an old two-story building, the backyard was a parking lot; workers fenced in the front so it served as a children's playground. Inside, there were several rooms downstairs. The communal living space shared by all clients included a large living room, dining room, kitchen, laundry and bath; there was an office and another room used as a private space for workers and clients to talk. There was a pay phone in the hall and bulletin boards throughout, which always were packed with announcements of community and shelter events; drawings by children were taped on most of the walls. Upstairs, there were five small bedrooms, each with a chest of drawers and two hospital beds. There was another bathroom and a large unfinished room used to store donations of clothes and belongings of clients.

While there were ongoing efforts to make this facility attractive, nothing managed to turn it into something remotely resembling a comfortable home or a decent hotel. The building was in structurally poor condition, plumbing problems were never-ending as were infestations of cockroaches and mice. In brief, the prime organizational resource was the facility itself, a place looking like an emergency hotel. Similar to emergency hotels in general, the shelter supplied clients with sheets, towels, toothbrushes, toothpaste, soap and shampoo, the availability of food and clothing depended on donations. The resource in most short supply was money, the only money available was from the few clients who did manage to pay the one dollar a day suggested rent.

The program designers who secured this facility and funding also constructed both the organizational philosophy and methods of service provision that did not change much over the time of my data collection. First of all, this was an organization with particular service goals. Recall that the collective representation of a battered woman is of a woman who needs and wants to achieve her independence; South Coast designers translated this into the *organizational goal*. According to the formal manual of operations, this place was to:

help women and children in violent family situations improve the quality of their lives, specifically to help women develop a sense of worth while they are achieving independence and self-sufficiency.

Also according to the formal manual of operations, South Coast was an alternative organization differing from traditional agencies, which assume a battered woman requires professional assistance. Again, according to the formal manual of operations:

> The shelter operates from the philosophical base that women are strong within themselves. The staff lends its strength to women in crisis to help them help themselves become independent and responsible for their decisions and actions. . . . The residents assist each other in building self-esteem which results in women learning to take control of their own lives.

Recall that the collective representation of shelters constructed the battered woman as a victim needing to increase faith in herself, something to be accomplished through self-help and peer support. According to the South Coast formal statement of service philosophy, this was to be the method of assisting such a woman within this place. The image here was of the client—always called either a "resident" or a "guest"—as a strong woman; the image was of women residing here helping one another.

The organization of daily life inside this place also was designed by the original planners and changed little during the time I collected my data. Each client was responsible for herself and for her children, each was responsible for her share of communal housekeeping chores, which were assigned on a rotating basis. Formal services were defined as housing and "advocacy," or help with negotiating the bureaucratic maze of area social service agencies. But advocacy was to be limited. The manual instructed "self-sufficiency is the key here. The secret is not to do for the woman, but to help her do for herself." Formal counseling also was not available inside this place.[4] If clients were interested, they were referred to local counselors who specialized in the problems of the battered woman.

That South Coast was specifically organized for the battered woman also is obvious in how workers justified organizational rules for clients' behaviors. True, workers deemed some rules as simply necessary to maintain the place: Each client was responsible for her children, for keeping her own sleeping area clean, for her own laundry and cooking as well as for her assigned share of the communal housekeeping chores.

Most rules, though, were justified as necessary and good for the battered woman type of person.

Several rules for client behavior were justified by workers as necessary for a woman in a situation of continuing, extreme danger. The prime organizational rule was about location confidentiality—clients could not tell anyone where South Coast was located; they certainly could not have guests at this place. Since workers believed clients were not safe on the streets at night, there also was a curfew rule. Further, there was a rule that clients needed advance permission to maintain their shelter residence while spending a night elsewhere. Again, workers said they worried whenever a client was outside South Coast, especially for an extended time. Finally, there was a rule of a three-day minimum stay with no contact with outsiders during this time. According to workers, this was necessary because, "when you get a woman who's been battered, the situation is so bad they need this time to get cooled off and feel safe." So, there were a variety of rules each justified by the construction of the battered woman as a woman in a situation of continuing, extreme danger.[5]

Other rules were justified in terms of what was needed for a battered woman to "get in touch" with her feelings. For example, there were rules requiring clients to participate in support groups. These were semiformal meetings workers said were important in order to educate clients, and to encourage them to escape their isolation and share their feelings. Sometimes at these meetings there would be guest lecturers talking about "wife abuse" and the "battered woman"; most often there would be worker-led discussions of the "feelings that accompany being battered." And, there was a rule prohibiting clients from consuming alcohol or illegal drugs inside *or* outside South Coast. According to workers, these substances "cut off feelings," and a battered woman is a woman who "needs to get in touch with what she's feeling."

Finally, there was an unwritten but implicit rule: clients must become involved in shelter life. Workers simply did not allow clients to spend the majority of their time in their bedrooms away from others, and they tended to become angry when a client spent the majority of her time away from South Coast. Workers claimed it was necessary for each woman to participate in shelter life because "this is a household where women help women."

In brief, South Coast was organized specifically for the battered woman, a type of woman needing only a good environment encouraging self-help and peer support, a type of woman capable of self-determination, a type of woman seeking to achieve independence from abuse. Although the collective representation of shelters would not lead us to expect rules for client behavior, it remains that all rules in this place were made justifiable in terms of what clients—the battered woman—needed.

While thus far I have painted an image of South Coast that is very similar to the image of shelters in their collective representation, such an image, of course, is far too idealized.

Collective representations, administrators, and workers at South Coast

> The people you get with CETA seem to have so many problems that sometimes it seems like they should be residents, not staff.
> Family Violence Program Administrator

> I feel like there's a big gap between the shelter and the FVP staff. I kept thinking last week throughout that meeting, it was terrible. Here all these people are sitting here and everything they talk about, it pales against what we have to go through.
> Shelter Worker

Ideally, shelters would be autonomous organizations run by the clients themselves. Within such an image, there would be no administrators or workers. Yet this certainly does not describe shelters in general or South Coast in particular.

The collective representation of shelters bracketed the practical issue of money for operations: Where will the money come from to buy or rent the shelter facility? Who will pay the phone and utility bills? While we might imagine a perfect world in which resources simply appeared, shelters in the United States from their beginning have been funded through various local, state, and federal government units, by churches and by organizations such as the United Way. While again we might imagine a perfect world in which agencies simply give money without placing restrictions on its use and without demanding accountability, in the practical world money comes with various stipulations. So it was with South Coast.

During the time I collected my data, the shelter received funding from the county and CETA, yet it was to be administered by the FVP. The story of relationships between South Coast and the FVP is complicated since, for the most part, their funding sources differed. The link between the two was a FVP staff position, "Family Services Delivery Manager," a person responsible for the shelter *and* for organizing other forms of community support for victims of wife abuse. Technically, the shelter coordinator reported to the Family Services Delivery Manager, who, in turn, reported to the FVP director. She, in turn, reported to various boards of directors, the county and the LEAA, the primary source of FVP funding.

One notable influence of the relationship between South Coast and the FVP was in the shelter's standing in the local community. For example, prior to its FVP connection, South Coast had a very hostile relationship with the local criminal justice system. But after being taken over by the FVP, supportive links were established. Workers developed a very good working relationship with police, police became a resource available to workers. On the other hand, there was continual pressure on workers to "encourage" clients to prosecute incidents of wife abuse and there were several incidents when police literally dumped off a woman at the South Coast door in the middle of the night.

South Coast's relationship with the FVP also encouraged links between the shelter and other community services such as welfare, housing, child welfare, and legal aid. On one hand, South Coast became enmeshed in this network, which at times compromised client confidentiality. For example, workers were trained to watch for instances of child abuse; they became susceptible to the advice offered by professional social service providers. At the same time, shelter clients, because they were shelter clients, qualified for immediate food stamps, their names went to the top of the list for county housing subsidies, a call from a shelter representative could yield somewhat quick response time for appointments with other agencies.

For the good, the bad, and the indifferent, South Coast was not an autonomous organization. But this story of interference in shelter affairs must be matched by the opposite story: South Coast suffered from administrative neglect.

Shelter workers themselves did not attend the weekly FVP staff meetings. While they were represented there by the shelter coordinator, it was clear in the early meetings that the routine operation of the shelter was not a priority for the FVP. After one meeting, the shelter coordinator expressed her anger at the perceived results of this administrative neglect:

> All my staff don't feel like they are getting any support from central staff. Do you know that last week (one of the central staff) asked me where the shelter *is*? I hear the component reports and I know they're involved in the program but in the last two or three weeks I haven't said a word, no one asked me how the shelter was doing. I've been shut off. We're having problems in the shelter, too, you know?

There were commonsense reasons behind such perceived neglect. First, FVP and shelter workers were dissimilar types of people. Central staff were administrators, planners, coordinators, and program designers; they were professionals while shelter workers never identified themselves in that way. Second, the shelter was not a critical component of FVP services. The LEAA funding for the FVP was directed primarily toward changing the criminal justice system; the shelter was important basically because LEAA wanted a "comprehensive strategy." Bluntly stated, the shelter was to be a resource for the criminal justice system. So, of all the FVP staff, only the Family Services Delivery Manager had any need for a practical understanding of shelter operations and, without exception, she was the only one to regularly go there. This was understandable. When FVP staff *did* go to South Coast there could be problems. For example, for a short time one FVP staff member was the formal trainer of shelter workers. This did not last because this person apparently knew only the collective representation of the battered woman and not the realities of shelter work. One worker offered me an empirical example to justify her evaluation that these formal training sessions had been worthless:

> They're gonna tell us about battered women? The presentation started by reading us the letter from a battered wife in Del Martin's book. It was like we didn't know anything.

In the first few months of the FVP there were several times when problems between the shelter and FVP staff erupted into open conflict. The conflict always was the same: The shelter wanted assistance but the FVP would not give it. Then, it seemed efforts to resolve tensions stopped. The shelter coordinator at that time said to me, "Hell, the FVP people don't understand what we're doing, they're not interested. That's O.K. to be honest, we'd rather do it ourselves."

Thus, the day-to-day operation and management of South Coast, in practice, was in the hands of workers and their immediate supervisor. While there were formal administrative channels leading from these persons to the FVP, they were not all that important for issues of routine operation.

South Coast, in brief, was not similar to the image of shelters as autonomous organizations. Likewise, this organization had paid workers. Recall that within the collective representation of shelters there was little attention paid to workers since, theoretically, shelters would be run by clients and volunteers. South Coast did not manage to achieve this ideal. First, in practice, volunteers could not be counted on to be responsible for any of the twenty-one eight-hour shifts per week needed to keep this place always open. Volunteers often were college students who would leave after the semester ended, and disappear during finals week and school vacations. According to seasoned workers, volunteers also had little interest in the actual work:

> Volunteers want to go on calls and pick up battered women. They don't want to stay and clean and take care of kids who have head lice, they aren't interested in that.

Likewise, the organization found it could not rely on clients to do the work necessary to keep the place open. Typical of most shelters, South Coast offered only thirty days of services and workers believed it simply was unfair to ask clients to take much of their time to do organizational work. After all: "They have enough to do as it is in just thirty days, how can we ask them to run the place, too?" More critically, clients often simply *refused* to do organizational tasks.[6]

Since the practical world did not cooperate and offer this organization free labor, paid workers were needed. Given workers formally needed no specific skills, and given they did not wield formal power, it was sensible for this organization, like many other such places at the time, to rely on CETA funding to pay frontline workers. By definition, women who qualified for CETA jobs were not professionals. During the time of my data collection, a total of fourteen women worked at South Coast, with anywhere from one to eight of them employed at the same time. Only a few of these women had education beyond high school, and only a few of them had much in the way of *any* previous employment experience. The assumption that professionals were not needed carried through to the shelter coordinator, a direct service worker herself, who also was the immediate supervisor of frontline workers. During the time of my data collection, there were three women who variously held this position. One of these women did not have a high school diploma, the other two did have four-year college degrees but neither of them had any specific professional credentials nor much in the way of previous experience in social services.

Relying on CETA funding to pay frontline workers had several consequences. When the CETA program first started, there were many people who potentially were eligible, but since a person lost CETA-eligibility after a year's employment, there were fewer and fewer women over time who qualified for employment, while the built-in maximum of one year eligibility fostered worker turnover. By the end of the third year of operation, it took a great deal of time, energy, and advertising to find *any* candidate for an open job. The coordinator at that time summarized her frustrations:

> I feel in hiring I have very few options. It's not like I have seven candidates for one job opening. I have maybe one candidate if I can scrape her up somewhere and one job opening so I don't feel like I have a lot of choice in who is hired.

As a consequence, South Coast most often was understaffed and there could be little filtering of potential employees through tests of their understandings of wife abuse or the battered woman. Indeed, I was on a hiring panel for one woman who became a worker and her first question to us was, "What I don't understand is why do these women stay?" Since the collective representation of the battered woman furnishes answers to this question, it is safe to assume she was not familiar with it and hence, did not begin work understanding the philosophy or mission of South Coast. So, coordinators and administrators could not assume new workers held organizationally compatible understandings of the client; they could not even assume workers freely chose South Coast as an employment site since, by definition, CETA workers were women who needed a job.

From the beginning, organizational supervisors and administrators attempted to train workers in how they should think about the battered woman and shelter work. Weekly training sessions were led by shelter coordinators, FVP administrators, and representatives of local social service agencies. Yet none of these persons ever claimed success in transmitting preferred images to workers. On the contrary, administrators and supervisors continually complained about worker heterogeneity. According to one shelter coordinator, for example, her present staff was not united in the image of how the shelter should be run: "One wants to run it like an army camp, another wants to run it like a commune." Another coordinator at another time complained that her workers were not united in their images of which women should receive services:

> Some workers are real hesitant to bring in a woman with lots of problems and lots of kids, but others are what you might call soft touches, they want to bring in everyone, the more problems, the better.

In brief, frontline workers posed problems for this organization. But just as clearly, South Coast posed problems for workers. Bluntly stated, shelter work was not a good job. CETA formally was about job training, but the general social service skills learned by workers were not likely to catapult them into future high paid employment. Furthermore, the pay was only slightly above minimum wage, the employment contract was for one year only. For this low pay and no job security, workers were assigned to revolving shifts, for example, they might work one day, then perhaps the following evening, then perhaps the following overnight; they each worked three out of every four weekends. To add further problems, there often were too few workers, so those who were off duty could be called in to handle emergencies. One administrator who saw herself and the shelter as feminist worried about the contradictions:

> They're working for a feminist organization that is basically screwing them over. You're a worker and you're not paid enough to live

on and you've worked six days in a row and on your day off you have to come in to a staff meeting. . . . Then, you go home and it's still your day off and you get a backup call and you have to go out.

We certainly are a long way from the collective representation image of shelters as places containing only "women supporting women." Shelter work at South Coast was a job, a job to be done within an organization.

Collective representations and organizational decision-making

> Negotiations always take place within social settings. The various structural conditions of the settings affect the actions of the negotiating partners, the aims they pursue . . . and undoubtedly, the outcomes of the negotiations themselves.
>
> Anselm Straus, *Negotiations*

Formally, all South Coast workers were powerless. Yet, like all "street-level" bureaucrats, they wielded considerable informal power. The discretion and autonomy associated with frontline workers in all social service agencies was magnified by two particular characteristics of South Coast.

First, formally this was not a rule-bound organization. Yes, as I have discussed, there were many rules on-the-record. But formally, no rule carried any specific sanction and the primary rule was that all rules were negotiable. The final statement on the house policies document signed by all new clients was clear: "Each case is evaluated individually, and exceptions to rules may be made depending upon the situation." Formally, then, it was not the job of workers to "enforce rules"; it was their job to be sensitive to the particular characteristics and needs of individual clients. In this way, workers were to be organizational negotiators, persons explicitly charged with making particularistic decisions reflecting the specific case at hand.

Second, worker power was magnified by a lack of supervision. Since the shelter always was open, although the coordinator was physically present only during week days, decisions most often were made while one or maybe two workers were on duty without supervision.

Relatively few decisions could be put off until the coordinator was contacted or returned to work so whoever was on duty had the power—and the necessity—of making decisions on behalf of the organization. In practice, this was the power to admit a new client or to deny a potential client entry, to decide what needed to be handled at house meetings, to decide when one or another rule should be suspended or referenced and if referenced, what sanctions were called for. Sure, in theory there were formal lines of authority but in practice, South Coast often belonged to whichever worker happened to be on duty when a decision had to be made. Thus, underlying the formal image of these workers as powerless there was very real power over clients.

However, it would be unwise to stop here and offer a mistaken image of these workers as free agents who could make any decision and take any action they personally desired. On the contrary. Although workers rarely saw one another except at their weekly meetings, they were engaged in a common enterprise—decisions made by one of them could affect them all. Just as critically, although these workers did develop a common culture, they could not have developed just any culture. As organizational representatives, there were organizational determinants to their decisions and actions. Only some resources were available, only some things were possible given the particular organizational design. South Coast was an organization for the battered woman, the result of the social problems work of translating collective images into organizational form.

Summary

Unlike lower-level workers in most organizations, street-level bureaucrats have considerable discretion in determining the nature, amount, and quality of benefits and sanctions provided by their agencies.

Michael Lipsky, *Street-Level Bureaucracy*

South Coast organizers attempted to make this an organization specifically for the battered woman. As will become increasingly clear in the next chapters, organizational goals, rules, and worker activity were justifiable only for this type of woman. Regardless, it also is clear that South Coast could not be described as a "classic exemplar" of a shelter for the battered woman. The organization's practical need for money led it to become involved with the FVP and hence to lose autonomy; its practical need for workers led it to become an employment site where workers had very real, if informal, power over their clients. In brief, the social problems work of translating a collective representation of "shelters for the battered woman" into a concrete organization called "South Coast" was accomplished within practical limitations, and an exemplar of the collective representation was not achieved. This is a general point: When social problems work fails to translate collective ideals into practical form, it can be due, in part, to the practical world failing to cooperate. What is bracketed in vague and abstract collective representations—in this case, an organization's need for money and workers—cannot be so bracketed in experience. The practical consequence is that social problems work of actually helping a client—in this case, a battered woman—will take place both within collective representations of what particular types of organizations should do, as well as within the world of myriad practical limitations informing the organizational structure.

My second point from this discussion about the organization of South Coast is that work within this place had organizational determinants. The organization furnished workers with some resources while it simultaneously set a variety of constraints on what was possible for them to achieve. It was within this particular organizational framework that workers were to actually accomplish shelter work. They were to go out into the world of complexity and ambiguity and select women as clients, they were to respond to these women in ways transforming them into strong and independent women, and, as practical actors, workers had to make sense of these activities. This all is social problems work, which, within South Coast, was characterized by considerable worker discretion while bounded by organizational characteristics.

I now will move from the relatively abstract statements of organizational form and philosophy into the messy world of practical experience. The first question is about selecting shelter clients: What was encompassed within this task of client selection and how could workers make sense of this practical activity?

Chapter Four

Identifying the Battered Woman

It is our interest at hand that motivates all our thinking, project-
ing, acting and therewith establishes the problems to be solved
by our thought and the goals to be attained by our actions.
Alfred Schutz, *On Phenomenology and Social Relations*

In turning to an examination of shelter work from the perspective
of those doing this work, it is important to take heed of Schutz' comments. We enter a different world. Unlike social problems claims-makers who have the luxury of bracketing the messiness of practical experience, direct service workers must accomplish their work within lived
realities. Unlike social problems claims-makers who construct "types"
of persons, workers deal with individuals; unlike claims-makers whose
interests lie in convincing the public that a problem is at hand, direct
service workers are motivated by their desires to help individuals, to
make their jobs both meaningful and manageable, and to make sense of
their practical experience. Workers, in other words, must get through
their days and hopefully feel good about their efforts. Furthermore,
unlike organizational administrators whose job, among other things, is
to protect the organization by offering glowing evaluations to outsiders,
workers cannot gloss the experience of daily crises and troubles. Unlike
organizational administrators, workers cannot regularly retreat into a
quiet office to think, plan, or repair. Certainly, the perspectives and
interests of front line workers in social service agencies differ from
those of organizational administrators, outside evaluators, and social
problems claims-makers.

So, to enter the world of South Coast workers. I will start at the
commonsense beginning, the work of selecting clients. This practical

activity was located within a range of considerations; it was a task loaded with ambiguities, complexities, and indeterminancy; it was an activity requiring sensemaking.

The practicalities of client selection

> It's not that you don't want to help her, it's just who do you help?
>
> Shelter Worker

South Coast was a unique social service in its immediate area. It differed from two other places offering emergency housing—one of these places did not allow children, the second accepted any person with any problem, and residents there were expected to give the shelter proprietors any money they might have upon entry. In contrast, South Coast allowed children; it was specifically for the battered woman, and the nominal fee of a dollar a day rent routinely was waived. South Coast also differed from the local welfare hotel managed by the county. To live in that place required official certification of poverty; it was a locally well-known site of frequent robberies and rapes and there were no support services. In contrast, South Coast had no formal economic requirements for entry; the environment was safe and workers were available for support.

As a consequence, South Coast was the *only* option for many women in need of emergency housing and for others it was their most *attractive* option. Not surprisingly, South Coast received many requests for services *and* these requests came from women in many types of situations—only some of which even remotely resembled the problems of "wife abuse." For example, requests for shelter came from women evicted from their apartments, from women hitchhiking through town, from women released from jails or mental hospitals. All such petitioners for service had no where to go; they needed emergency housing. The practical task of client selection is understandable only against this background since, unlike workers in many agencies who receive their clients by professional referrals and thus are insulated by layers of organizational procedures,[1] most women requesting shelter were not screened. Each petitioner simply assumed, or at least hoped, a place advertised as a "shelter for battered women" could offer assistance.

Of course, there are myriad ways to cope with a high demand for services from women in diverse situations and with dissimilar problems and needs. From time to time workers tried the method of no client selection—any woman who wanted shelter could have it. But these times came only when a new group of workers replaced those with experience, such times always were short-lived. Each new group of workers rediscovered the negative practical consequences of admitting too many women or of admitting women with too many problems. Of course, it is easy to speculate about how workers themselves benefited from client selection, since this was one way for them to manage their work. But within this place, relying on communal living and peer support to achieve service goals, workers themselves talked of client selection as an unfortunate but necessary practice. Speaking from her experience, one worker told me that admitting too many women led other clients to declare the living arrangements simply unacceptable:

> I know from experience that when the shelter gets real crowded women start returning to their boyfriends because they can't stand it. They come in and say, "Oh, my God, it's overwhelming. I can't take this. I can't live this way." So, practically speaking, it doesn't work. You lose people you might otherwise benefit by bringing everyone in.

Another worker justified the practice of denying entry to women with too many problems for the same reason—it encouraged other clients to return to their violent relationships and therefore prevented service success:

> If you bring in someone who's, like violent, and disturbing other people, if they're off the wall and women are scared, they might go back to the battering man because at least they know what that's like versus living with a complete stranger you feel scared of and don't know what they might do.

Within the collective image of shelters, an overcrowded shelter does not matter, since clients are constructed as simply grateful to be away from their abuse. Within collective images, furthermore, there would not be women inside shelters who were frightening to others, since a battered woman type of person is anything but such a person. Yet these expectations did not fit the practical experience of South Coast workers, who learned the shelter environment *did* matter, and that this environment was something *to be created*. The practice of client selection was justified by workers in this way. It was practical activity oriented to maintaining an acceptable number of clients and to selecting appropriate clients, both of which were vague and often unobtainable goals.

On a day-to-day basis it was difficult to maintain an acceptable number of clients. While a "too full" shelter was associated with havoc, and while workers worried about wasting resources when the shelter was not "full enough," what specifically constituted "full" never was formally defined. Indeed, workers effectively resisted FVP efforts to place formal limits on the number of women and children who could be housed simultaneously. According to workers, "space availability" was totally situated, it depended on such things as the current mix of women and children, which women might share a bedroom, the specific characteristics of current clients and so forth.

In addition to this indeterminancy of what constituted "full," workers argued that it was immoral to turn away some women. These were women who contacted the shelter at night: "There's not much you can do if it's at night and she has nowhere else to go." In particular, this pertained to women who already had left their homes because of violence: "If it's at night and she's on the street, you have to think a long time about turning away a woman who's on the street because of battery." According to workers, such a woman should be granted immediate entry *regardless* of space availability. And, of course, no one could predict when such a woman might call. In contrast to claims constructing shelters as *always* full, there was an ebb and flow of requests to South Coast. At times—always unpredictable—the organization could not have met client demand if it had been twice its actual size; at other times—likewise unpredictable—there would be unused bedrooms for days at a time but no one would call requesting service. Since workers did not have control over the timing of requests for services, selection decisions occurred within this inability to predict future demand for services. This was further complicated by the unanimous understanding of workers that it was wrong to admit a woman and then ask her to leave if someone else seemed to be in more dire need of service. Workers talked of making a commitment with a selection decision to allow as much as a thirty-day maximum stay. Finally, workers could not predict when current clients would leave thus freeing space for others. In practice, it was common for women to remain longer than thirty days; it also was common for clients to announce they would be leaving only to have their plans fall through or to have a change of mind. So, workers often would assume a client would be leaving and they would admit a new client; assumed short-term overcrowding could become quite long-term.

I want to paint an image here of the messy practicalities of maintaining an acceptable number of clients. While workers often talked of their desires to do this, in practice, South Coast typically alternated between being too full and not full enough.

Workers also were oriented to selecting "appropriate" clients.[2] In practice, the meaning of this term shifted in relation to workers' evaluations of space availability. An "appropriate client" was a woman who workers felt *could be* and *should be* served given current "space availability." At the extreme, a "high priority client" was the "most appropriate client"; she was designated as a woman who should be served before all others regardless of space availability. Although the meaning of "appropriate client" thus shifted, the term could have at least five dimensions, each of which were commonsensically related to the practice of shelter work.

First and foremost, a woman was an appropriate client if she was judged to *need emergency housing*. When I asked workers what constituted "need," they offered several indications. For example, they said need was related to the immediacy of a petitioner's situation:

> For most women, the beatings have been going on for years, but if someone called and was in a threatening immediate situation, if someone was threatening them now, that would be a priority.

Need also was indicated when a petitioner was judged to have nowhere else to go:

> I give higher priority if she doesn't have any money. If she's got money she can go to a motel.

And, need was indicated when a woman had responsibilities for small children:

If she has children, especially small children, and is without resources, that's a priority.

Commonsensically, defining as "appropriate clients" those petitioners needing emergency housing made good sense. Why would service providers in a position to choose their clients select persons who did not need the primary organizational service? Furthermore, turning away a woman who seemed to need emergency housing was the most hated worker task. Simply stated: "No one wants to be responsible for turning away a woman who has nowhere else to go."

Second, workers labeled as "appropriate clients" those petitioners judged to *want the full range of South Coast services*. Most simply, workers distinguished South Coast from an emergency hotel and an appropriate client was a woman wanting more than a hotel. One worker was clear when she told me, "I tell them this is not the YWCA; this is not a hotel"; another said, "I tell them this is not a resort." Another said these were grounds for decisions to deny entry to petitioners:

> I don't want women who just need a place to stay. One woman I went to pick up, I didn't bring her in; she just wanted a place to crash.

Such a content of the appropriate client category is commonsensically understandable in a place where workers said, "the only difference between the shelter and a cheap hotel is our support services." If South Coast were used by women as a "place to crash," then what would be the jobs of workers? What would be the chance of forming a cohesive community of women? What would happen to service goals? So, it makes good sense that workers here defined as an "appropriate client" those petitioners who wanted what the organization had to offer.

Third, there was a motivation aspect to the notion of appropriate client. According to workers, the appropriate client would be a woman who needed housing and who wanted services for a *particular reason*:

> If they are unable to help themselves for any reason, that means we can't help them. Why should we try? Some women are afraid but they're not ready to be helped out of the situation.

The importance of "wanting to be helped out of the situation" was rephrased by another worker who said, "I'm more apt to admit someone who really wanted to make changes," and repeated by another when she said, "I try to find out who really wants to make a change and who's half-assed about it." In its most restrictive form, an appropriate client would be a woman whose personal goals matched the South Coast goal of assisting clients in becoming independent:

> I maintain that our services are best for women who want to make a break from their husbands.

This, too, makes good practical sense. Why would a service provider in any organization select clients whose personal goals differed from those of the organization? Common sense and practical experience leads to the prediction that service provision is the most effective—and pleasant for all concerned—when client and service provider agree on the goals to be accomplished.

Fourth, at South Coast an appropriate client was a woman who needed and wanted services *because she was a battered woman.* Although funding stipulations required this shelter to have a client category called "woman-in-transition," (women who need housing for any reason), workers unanimously argued that such a woman was an inappropriate client. First, there was no clear understanding of who belonged in this category so workers feared that such clients would make South Coast into a cheap hotel. According to one worker: "Do you realize how many women fit that category? How easy it would be to be a flophouse?" Second, they argued that the woman-in-transition category stretched organizational resources too far: "Are we primarily an agency to assist battered women or will we dilute our strength if we do this other thing?" Last but certainly not least, workers argued that South Coast was set up particularly for the battered woman and that organizational rules made no sense for "women who aren't running from violence and women who aren't trying to leave their boyfriends"; they argued they could not assist women-in-transition since "all our training has been about battered women." In brief, although there was a formally defined second priority client category called "women-in-transition," workers felt such a woman was different from the battered woman and therefore was inappropriate for shelter services. This, too, makes sense: South Coast was explicitly designed for the battered woman.

Fifth and finally, an appropriate client would be a woman deemed capable of living communally. Formal rules excluding women with chemical dependencies or recent histories of suicide attempts or psychiatric hospitalization each were twice justified in the formal manual of operations: The shelter did not have the capabilities to assist such women *and* their presence in the shelter might likely interfere with the goal of creating a supportive environment for all clients. Workers thus said, "I have to think about the women already here." Again, this is sensible. Like other shelters, South Coast placed much hope on the therapeutic power of the shelter environment. So, it is logical that workers would be oriented to the practicalities of establishing this environment. To do otherwise would risk reducing the quality of the environment deemed so important in resolving the problems of the battered woman type of person.

If all these worker constructions of the appropriate client were combined, a composite image would emerge and it would be an image of the battered woman—a woman who wanted and needed housing and services in order to become independent, a woman with personal characteristics compatible with this particular type of organization with these particular types of services. Thus, within a practical context of high demand for services from women in diverse situations, a social problem collective representation becomes a practical collective representation: "The battered woman" is also "the appropriate client."

While workers could talk about their notions of appropriateness, such talk did not describe the practical problems they encountered in actually selecting such a woman for services. Within the complex and multifaceted practicalities informing this task, the activity of actually choosing clients was anything but straightforward.

The practicalities of identification

A lot of women have been brought in inappropriately. One had psychiatric problems, another, whose husband wanted her to be here but she didn't want to, and one who came here because she didn't get along with anyone at home. She stayed for three days and ripped us off. Took off with a new wardrobe. That's my subjective interpretation.

Shelter Worker

It is one thing to claim these workers could construct an appropriate client as a woman with a particular constellation of personal characteristics. It would be quite another to claim they somehow went out into the world and chose such women for shelter residence. Workers themselves denied that the job of client selection was one of applying these notions of appropriate client to individual petitioners. While they could talk easily in terms of abstractions of what was important, they simultaneously denied these were criteria for entry. Within worker culture, three practicalities prevented an application of criteria. These were the problems of information, moralities, and heterogeneities.

First there was the problem of information. Since workers usually did not personally know women petitioning for service, they made decisions based on limited knowledge. In the extreme, workers might have *no* knowledge of a new client—some women entered this place sight unseen.[3] In the typical case, a woman would call once, twice, or even three times before deciding she wanted to pursue entry. A face-to-face meeting would be arranged with her in a public place. During this meeting, one or maybe two workers would decide whether or not she was appropriate, or, better stated, appropriate enough given the current space availability; the woman would decide whether or not she still wanted shelter entry.[4]

This decision-making was fraught with problems since worker culture transmitted many stories indicating that petitioners could be somewhat less than truthful in their desire to secure shelter. According to workers, you could not simply ask a woman if she was chemically dependent or otherwise ineligible: "They're not going to tell you that they have these problems." You could not necessarily believe a woman's story since "a lot of times you don't hear the real story until after they've been here," or "they'll tell you anything to get in here." Sure, workers understood the dire need of women for housing, and they constantly complained about the lack of services for women who needed them although, for one or another reason, they could not be served at South Coast. But practical experience could be disheartening and lead to distrust:[5]

> With some we've found this is a way of life for them. You aren't the
> only agency they've used. There are some that have been down this

road before, they know what they're doing. It's a shock when you first find out. We were naive. You resent it very much.

Second, there was the problem of moralities. The content of the collective representation of the battered woman and the philosophy of South Coast explicitly taught to these workers regularly confounded their decision-making. In particular, while it made good practical sense to deny women entry to a communal living arrangement if they were alcoholic, drug dependent, had recent histories of suicide attempts, or psychiatric hospitalization, the content of the battered woman collective representation made denial of entry a form of victim-blaming. Within the collective representation, such troubles are constructed as consequences of victimization. Since they are constructed as transient problems that disappear when a woman leaves her abusive relationship, such troubles do not matter to the practice of shelter work. This set of constructions led to countless debates among workers. For example, one worker in a staff meeting questioned the rule about alcohol use by relaying to others a challenge she had received:

> This girl that works in the grocery store down the street said, "I don't think it's right. Even if she's drunk she may be getting her ass beat." I said we try to find someplace else. That's a touchy question—if we are supposed to intervene with the violence, if she's drunk because he beats her or he beats her because she's drunk, we don't know.

A second worker then claimed that she, too, was hesitant to enforce this formal rule:

> I have no problem personally bringing someone into the shelter who was drinking or using drugs at the moment she entered if the battering incident just occurred. I'm not sure I wouldn't get drunk, quite frankly, 20 minutes after I got beat to hell.

At another meeting, a worker complained about the formal rule denying entry to women who had recent histories of suicide attempts:

> I think that a woman going through a traumatic situation like battery, if she's got kids, she's being battered, maybe she can't go out and work, hasn't worked, doesn't know—that's a hell of a situ-

ation and she might get desperate and think about killing herself, doing herself in.

Indeed, a shelter coordinator explicitly told workers in one training session to be hesitant about labeling a woman "crazy":

> . . . it's a real fine line in this kind of work we do and you have to keep in mind these women have been through a lot of trauma and they might appear like they're totally fucked up, out of their gourd. But that's not necessarily due to any brain tumor or the fact that they're psychotic. If you listen to their stories you'll see where it comes from, they may or may not be crazy. But you see it's real possible that wherever they're at is from what they've been through in terms of trauma.

This is the problem of moralities. Just as workers argued it was immoral to deny entry to a woman on the street at night because of wife abuse, they argued it was immoral to deny entry to a woman experiencing personal troubles from her abuse. Each worker's comment illustrates how the collective representation of the battered woman could neutralize troublesome characteristics formally preventing entry. Yet each worker's comment also demonstrates how this neutralization was bounded. That is, not *all* alcohol use, bizarre behavior, or suicide attempts automatically were forgiven. Rather, according to the logic of these comments, troublesome characteristics could be and should be neutralized only when they were caused by the condition known as "wife abuse." So, workers wanted to know "if she's drunk because he beats her *or* if he beats her because she's drunk"; they would have no problem allowing a woman to enter who had been drinking or using drugs "twenty minutes" after she "got beat to hell"; suicide attempts were understandable *if* a woman was in a "hell of a situation"; workers were to "listen carefully to their stories to see where the craziness comes from." Needless to say, such moralities behind decisions to exclude formally ineligible women greatly complicated the process of client selection.

Last but certainly not least, there was the problem of heterogeneity. The final worker decision on selection was dichotomous—a woman was allowed or denied entry, but there were multiple criteria pertaining to this decision. In practice, a given woman might be judged as obviously in need of shelter because of wife abuse, but she might object to living with women of varying races and social classes and/or she might exhibit problems judged as too severe to be assisted by this organization. Should she be admitted or not? Or, a woman might have money to go elsewhere but a worker might decide a motel would not give her the support she needed. Should she be granted entry or not? Or, a woman might be a lovely person and she might desire independence but only because she no longer liked her husband. What decision would be called for? I cannot enumerate all the possible combinations because that is my point: While the content of the battered woman/appropriate client category was homogeneous—a woman who needed *and* wanted housing *and* services *and* wanted them for particular reasons *and* had characteristics compatible with requirements for communal living—the characteristics of petitioners were far more heterogeneous. Hence, relatively few selection decisions were clear.[6]

In summary, according to workers, the practice of client selection involved the process of balancing multiple considerations within the context of faulty information. It could involve conflicting moralities where final evaluations were not clear and where evaluations depended on the situation inside South Coast at that moment as well as on the characteristics of the petitioner. Final decisions were consequential yet for this task workers had few guidelines and only vague, explicitly negotiable rules. They accomplished this task within a background of high ideals but within organizational limitations. Critically, responsibility for decisions most often fell to whichever worker happened to be on duty, so it was difficult to share guilt or blame with others.

While this paints a portrait of workers as individual decision-makers, they also were organizational representatives. They were engaged in the common task of shelter work, so it is to be expected that they would be held accountable for making these decisions appear logical, rational, and reasonable. That is my next question: Within this world of buzzing confusion, indeterminancy, complexities, and heterogeneities, how could workers make sensible their client selection decisions?

Categorizations and justifications

Crisis line with Margaret, who had been abused by her husband. She said husband came home drunk tonight and started yelling at her and kids. I told her we deal only with emergency physical abuse and since she only wanted shelter for one night, referred her to [another shelter].

Note in shelter log, day 655

As organizational representatives, workers were accountable for their client selection decisions. Accountability could be required by several types of audiences: The FVP, funding agencies, and the public. But here I am interested in accounts offered to an audience of *other workers*. At South Coast the shelter *logbook* was the place where workers offered accounts to one another for the full range of their organizational decisions and actions.[7] These log entries were written by workers and, since the log could be read only by workers, they show a view of accountability offered to organizational insiders.

The most common log entry surrounding decisions to *admit* a new client was of the simple form "brought in new resident, battered woman." Thus, the following type of entry was common:

Call on crisis line from Dora, battered woman. Brought her in.

[413]

Likewise, although South Coast had the client category of woman-in-transition, a common entry surrounding a decision to *deny* a woman shelter was of the simple form, "she was not a battered woman." The following entries, for example, both were made on days when there was no problem with space availability:

[hospital] called. Wanted to dump a woman on us because she had no place to go. She wasn't a battered woman, referred to [another shelter].

[470]

Woman called on crisis line, has not been battered but landlord threw her out. . . . We should not let her in since she is not battered.

[744]

Within South Coast, a label given to petitioners could be sufficient in and of itself to justify workers' client selection decisions. In theory, then, South Coast was for the battered woman; in practice, this label for an individual woman could be sufficient to justify a decision to admit her while a label of "not-battered" could be sufficient in and of itself to justify a decision to exclude her.

Given this association between labels and worker justifications, the task becomes one of examining the grounds upon which workers attached labels to individual women. Of course, in the examples already given there were no grounds—petitioners simply were labeled as a "battered woman," or as a "not-battered woman." But other log entries show something of the grounds workers offered one another to support their labels. This is a complicated puzzle so I will examine it from several perspectives.

First, since notions of "appropriateness" shifted with the changing condition inside South Coast, I will hold the situation constant by examining entries made during *one* night shift. On this particular night, South Coast already was quite full so the on duty worker would have been using relatively stringent criteria for allowing another woman to enter. This worker made two log entries noting that she had received three requests for shelter during this shift. The first entry was very brief and told others that during this time two women had been *denied* shelter:

> Two calls from women needing one night place to sleep. Referred to [another shelter] and cheap motels.
>
> [399]

The second entry pertained to a woman who was *admitted*:

> Call on crisis line from police. Gale, was kicked out of her home, battered many times previously and went to police.
>
> [399]

Typical of log notations in general, these notes are very short. They gave others no details on how these events transpired. What is of interest is what these entries *do* contain. The first, surrounding decisions to refer women elsewhere, only mentions that two women—both nameless—had called and each requested housing for one night. No details are given about why these women requested housing, evaluators know only that they wanted to use South Coast as an emergency hotel. Contrast this with the second entry justifying the decision to admit a woman to this place. Here the woman is named and in two short sentences evaluators learn (1) the call came from the police, indicating that whatever had happened was serious enough to involve law enforcement; (2) the woman was without a place to live; (3) she had been battered many times previously. On-the-record, these entries portray a worker making sensible decisions: During the night she had offered shelter to a battered woman type of person and she had deflected two "not-battered" types of persons.

Regardless of what these petitioners might have said during their conversations with the on duty worker, on-the-record, these three selection decisions were made sensible, logical, rational, and justifiable in terms of the *client*. This is the social problems work of justifying selection decisions, the worker activity that can be examined from a second perspective. Again, I will hold constant the condition inside this place. This time I will examine the progressive entries constructing one woman. On this day, too, South Coast was quite full. Entries are in the order of their appearance:

> Woman called, staying in motel and can't afford it for too much longer. Told her we were full and suggested [another shelter].

> Susan (motel woman) called back and she is really desperate. She has four children (4, 3, 2, 1) and no transportation. She said she would stay in motel but cannot afford it.

> 8:30 P.M. Susan called. Needs shelter badly, has four children, husband searching for her. She's been battered and is frightened—requires shelter till she can relocate. Called [another worker] and we think we should pick her up.

> [658]

Again, only two workers actually talked with this woman, others knew only what was written in the log. On-the-record, Susan was constructed over the course of the day. She began as a nameless woman wanting an alternative to living in a motel. She progressed to a named woman who was desperate, had children, and could not afford to remain in the motel. Finally, she is constructed as a battered woman type of person—a woman who was frightened and in danger, a woman wanting to remain independent from her abusive partner, and therefore, a woman who could not be turned away. Of course, it is quite possible that Susan identified herself as a "battered woman" during the first phone call, it also is quite possible she changed her story with each call. Regardless, what appeared on the record were only those characteristics justifying workers' decisions. The first entry justified a decision to deflect her, the second was ambiguous and put workers on notice that perhaps a new decision was called for, and the third justified the decision to admit her.

This is social problems work, the activity of justifying organizational decisions. At South Coast, this could be accomplished through workers' use of the battered woman collective representation as an interpretive scheme. Out of all petitioners might have said about themselves what ended up on-the-record were only those characteristics pertaining to this type of person. Since these simultaneously were the characteristics of the "appropriate client," this particular scheme of interpretation furnished grounds for justifying the sensible nature of client selection decisions. What was accomplished along the way, of course, was that individual clients were each constructed as one of two types of people, either they were a "battered woman" or they were a "not-battered woman."

This raises a question: What are the characteristics of these two types of people as understood by workers? This is an unanswerable question. Like any interpretive scheme, the "battered woman" collective representation is open-ended; what mattered was not the presence or absence of any one characteristic; what mattered was their relationship to one another, the gestalt impression.

In order to demonstrate the importance of the gestalt images created by workers in their accounts to one another, I will look at log entries in a third way. This time I will use examples that hold constant worker noted characteristics of petitioners. Using several parallel examples, I want to illustrate how individual characteristics mattered only as they stood in relation to the gestalt image created by the worker. As a first example, recall that in formal interviews workers said a woman who had "someplace else to go" could be justifiably excluded. Consider such an account as it appeared in the log:

> Hotline call from Joyce, rather evasive, claims to battery (husband), has three children—husband has kicked her out of the house, refuses

to let her return. Joyce requested a place to sleep for 2-3 days. She's employed. I do not see an immediate need here—she has mother and friends here.

[655]

The final worker justification for a decision to deny entry was that Joyce had someplace else to go. But this did not stand in isolation. The final justification came after and therefore stood in relation to the previous characterizations. And, as constructed, Joyce was not a battered woman type of person in any way. In a few short sentences, the worker constructed her as a not appropriate client because she probably was not a "battered woman" (*claims* to battery), on the grounds that (1) she was not trapped (kicked out); (2) she did not want shelter services (a place to sleep); (3) she was not economically dependent (employed); and (4) she was not isolated from others (mother, friends). Regardless of what Joyce might have said during this conversation, she was constructed as a "not-battered woman/not appropriate client" in *all* ways. Having someplace else to go was merely the final and formal justification, which was a sensible ground for exclusion *given all else*.[8]

Now, compare the construction of Joyce with that of Barbara, a woman who also called when the shelter was quite full. Barbara received entry although the worker characterized her as a woman who *did* have someplace else to go:

I received a crisis call from Barbara. Her husband hit her three times in the past year, last night was the last time. She's too ashamed to go to friends but she wants to be independent of husband. I stressed the point of going to friends but she was adamant about her embarrassment. I told her we were full, but could work something out.

[642]

Is this not a description of a battered woman type of person? The worker constructed the call as urgent (crisis) and she constructed the woman as one who (1) had experienced repeated violence; (2) had just experienced violence; (3) wanted to be independent, but (4) was too ashamed about her plight to call on her friends for help. *Within this image created by the worker*, this woman's alternatives to South Coast were neutralized. Since she could not make use of alternatives for the *particular reason* that she was embarrassed, it did not matter that she had some place else to go. Barbara was constructed as a typical battered woman type of person. In brief, the characteristic of having some place else to go mattered only if the petitioner was in other ways seeable as a "not-battered woman."

I shall use a second example to illustrate the importance of gestalt images. Recall that workers said South Coast was an *emergency* shelter, and at times they could use this to deflect women who were constructed as not in immediate danger:

> [another worker] knows Karen who has applied for shelter admission. She thinks she should be ineligible. I agree, she hasn't been hit in two years anyway.
>
> [436]

This cryptic entry does not say why the other worker thought Karen should be ineligible, but that does not matter. The worker writing the entry constructed her own justification which *explicitly* stood in relation to other grounds for ineligibility. Karen might or might not have been ineligible but "she hasn't been hit in two years *anyway.*" The characteristic of not experiencing immediate physical abuse takes on its importance in relation to some other—unexplained—"ineligibility."

Compare this with another entry, one supporting a decision to admit a new client constructed as a woman who might not have *ever* experienced physical abuse. Yet she was admitted and indeed, she received the worker label of *very typical* battered woman.

> . . . She has been mentally abused by her husband for about three years. Her doctor told her to get out before it's too late. She sounds like a very typical battered woman. She can not do anything, has lost all her friends, is always at home living this way. Her doctor told her that her physical problems are due to stress and will get better when she leaves him. She has been warned not to tell him she's leaving.
>
> [518]

Is this not a battered woman type of person? Granted, she was not constructed as a physically abused woman, but she was one whose "mental abuse" had been long lasting, a woman suffering physical health problems from the abuse, a woman who was helpless and friendless. Furthermore, the note constructed this woman's husband as an abusive man because others thought he was dangerous; they had warned her not to tell him she was leaving. Within this image created by the worker, it did not matter that this woman had not experienced physical abuse because she was the same type of person—she was a "battered woman." In brief, the characteristic of not experiencing physical abuse mattered only if the gestalt created by the worker was of a "not-battered woman."

I shall add complexity. Just as a woman could be constructed as a battered woman type of person although she had *not* suffered physical abuse, she could be constructed as a not-battered type of person even though she *had* been physically assaulted. The following entry occurred on a day when there was plenty of space. Although the note conveyed worker hesitancy about the appropriateness of this label, it justified a decision to admit a "battered woman."

> Brought in Madge. She seems to fit more in the category of woman-in-transition than battered woman, although she has been hit by her boyfriend. Madge is married and her husband lives in Pittsburg. Madge has a boyfriend who she is traveling with who dumped her here. The boyfriend has beaten her before but Madge's prime concern now is to get back to Pennsylvania.
>
> [828]

Was Madge a "battered woman?" Well, she had been hit and she had been beaten before, but this note conveyed a worker's hesitation that such experiences made her truly a "battered woman." Such a woman, after all, is not a woman who travels with a boyfriend, a woman who wants to get back to her husband. So, the characteristic of experiencing physical assault was neither necessary nor sufficient to be incorporated into the category of "battered woman." What mattered was the gestalt image created by the worker.

At South Coast, the gestalt of a "battered woman" or a "not-battered woman" could be created by any two or more characteristics associated with these types of people. There was no list of characteristics deemed always relevant to these constructions. In the final analysis, each petitioner presented a unique constellation of characteristics so no two gestalts were the same.[9]

Regardless of the buzzing confusion they encountered, workers themselves could make their decisions rational, logical, and defensible to one another by their use of the battered woman interpretive scheme, which was simultaneously the appropriate client scheme. On-the-record, workers demonstrated to one another that they each were representatives of a shelter for the battered woman. This is social problems work. After all, workers did not confront a world where petitioners came neatly sorted into organizational categories, so it was worker activity that brought the heterogeneity of social life into line with the homogeneity of collective representations. What all accounts shared is that the organizational bases for decision-making, the ambiguities, confusions, complexities, and indeterminancies surrounding selection decisions simply disappear. What mattered on-the-record was only the final classification—was this woman a "battered woman" or not? South Coast was for the "battered woman" and on-the-record, such a woman achieved entry.

Commonsense interpretations, categorizations, and justifications

> When you're talking to people, you get vibes, it's a sixth sense, you get vibes "this woman is lying to me." You have to start slowing down until you can determine what's going on. The hard thing is to determine the source of the vibes so you can make some kind of decision.
>
> Shelter Worker

Although South Coast workers could use the "battered woman/appropriate client" interpretive scheme to justify their client selection decisions, this device nonetheless relied on folk reasoning. This folk reasoning guided the practical work of *evaluating*, the task intervening between what workers said were the characteristics of "appropriate" or "inappropriate" clients and the ways they constructed individual petitioners. Actual petitioners, of course, were heterogeneous in their characteristics, so the neat and tidy gestalt images were worker constructions. As such, there still is the question of how workers created such constructions out of the heterogeneity of actual petitioners' stories and characteristics.

Sociologically, we would say that workers created these images when they wrote accounts for their selection decisions. We might agree with C. Wright Mills and argue that workers made decisions and *then* constructed grounds upon which to justify decisions to others.[10] This certainly is logical since we would expect the complex stories told by most petitioners would give workers enough evidence to construct *either* of the two gestalt images. If so, then underlying the use of the collective representation of the battered woman in accounting would be whatever folk methods of identification and classification that happened to be used by whichever individual worker was making the decision.

And this is how workers themselves talked of the process of client selection. When I asked them how they actually made these decisions, they would go no further than saying, "It's just done on instinct," "You get a sixth sense," or "vibes, it's done on vibes." In use, "vibes" or "instinct" or "sixth sense" were shorthand expressions to label the end result of myriad and interlocking subjective assessments. Thus, when workers talked with me in formal interviews or when they talked informally among themselves, the folk reasoning underlying their decisions was obvious. For example, I asked how they knew when to believe a woman's story and one worker replied: "You learn to read what they don't say." Another said, "some things you just know." When talking among themselves, one worker asked another why a particular woman was denied entry and the worker making the decision said, "Her story didn't sound right." When I asked how they knew a woman was motivated to make a change in her life, one worker said, "You learn to tune into reluctance, uncertainties." At another time a petitioner was constructed as "mentally ill" and the worker making this construction said, "I knew she was a shakey person. I knew because she wouldn't tell us anything about herself."

Since these workers developed the common understanding that "vibes" could not be specified, they rarely talked about the actual process whereby they came to construct one or another gestalt image of a petitioner. Furthermore, since they allowed one another to justify client selection decisions by labels without grounds, the shelter log contained few hints of how workers pieced together gestalt images.[11] Yet it remains: although the grounds for labeling petitioners were most typically glossed, underlying the neat and tidy categorization system provided by the battered woman interpretive scheme was commonsense folk reasoning. The device thus disguised this underlying reasoning yet nonetheless relied on it.

Summary

> Institutions bestow sameness. Socially based analogies assign disparate items to classes and load them with moral and political content.
>
> Mary Douglas, *How Institutions Think*

Within the world of practical experience, people and events are heterogeneous, and there are practical constraints on human action. Regardless, it was the task of South Coast workers to select women to become official members of the battered woman social collectivity. From the organizational viewpoint, it was their task to select "appropriate" shelter clients.

Readers who are outsiders to shelter work might criticize these workers and ask: What gave them the right to deflect shelter entry because the "vibes" were not right? What gave them the right to turn away women who requested only housing for one night? What gave them the right to make such invidious distinctions among women who all needed housing? If workers' practical experience and organizational position are not kept in focus, then this examination could be read as an example of the capricious use of power by street-level bureaucrats. Obviously, it certainly is true that it took far more than being hit and/or needing housing for a woman to be admitted to South Coast; it is true that it was workers' distinctions and decisions that led to many women being turned away. But to stop here would lead to the belief that "better workers," or perhaps "professional workers" would have made different kinds of distinctions and decisions. Not necessarily true. Within the perspectives and experiences of workers, distinctions among women *had to be made*, and not just for the purpose of controlling the number of clients. South Coast—or *any* social service for that matter—could be made infinitely larger yet some—many—petitioners would remain "inappropriate" for services. Simply stated, a given organization cannot be all things to all people. Once there is an organizational structure, once there are formal service goals then, ipso facto, only some people can be assisted.

In the case at hand, South Coast was organized specifically to assist women of the battered woman type. The necessity for workers' distinctions among women follows from the organizational design, which made a "battered woman" the "appropriate client": A woman who wanted and needed what the organization had to offer, and a woman who would become a good member of the shelter community of women. The fact that workers *had* to make distinctions arises from the disjunctures between the clear and internally logical package of social problems claims linking "wife abuse," "the battered woman," "shelters," and the heterogeneity of lived realities which are, of course too numerous to innumerate: Some women wanted/needed housing but had not experienced "wife abuse"; some women had experienced "wife abuse" but did not want to "achieve independence"; some women did not have the personal skills or desires to live communally and so on. Likewise, workers' use of folk reasoning to make distinctions among women follows from the fact that there is no x-ray, no test to determine which real women are instances of the "battered woman/appropriate client." Thus, workers could only look for signs and try to "match" the perceived characteristics of individual women with the collective representation of the "battered woman," which simultaneously was the representation of the "appropriate client." These workers were not necessarily experts in understanding the characteristics associated with the battered woman. They were, however, practical actors who quickly learned that this was the type of woman who could be served, the type of woman who should be served, the type of woman likely to become a good client and a good member of the shelter community of women.

In brief, the practical need for these *particular* distinctions among women stems from the organizational framework which, in turn, stems from the collective representations of "wife abuse" and the "battered woman." Thus, what social problems claims-makers accomplish rhetorically—distinguishing all troubles from "wife abuse," distinguishing all victimized women from the "battered woman"—workers accomplished in fact. The practical consequence of their discriminations and decisions was that only some women were allowed entry to South Coast and hence, only some women became official members of the battered woman social collectivity. This is social problems work, the moral and political work of assigning some women—and only some women—to the class of persons called the "battered woman."

This also is the social problems work of accounting for the sensible nature of organizational decisions. In worker talk about selection and in their accounts to one another for particular selection decisions, they displayed their understanding that "appropriate" clients—battered women—had achieved entry, and that "not appropriate" clients—not-battered women—had been deflected. The world thus was practically and rhetorically divided into two types of people. Women were "battered" or "not-battered"; all heterogeneity disappeared. So, regardless of how these petitioners differed among themselves, on-the-record all new clients were instances of the same type of person: the "battered woman."

Of course, such neat and tidy descriptions of new clients were a construction of workers who heard complicated stories and balanced myriad and often conflicting indications of a petitioner's status; they were non-definable gestalt images created by worker "vibes." Given this, it seems safe to say that the homogeneity among women allowed South Coast entry was an artifact produced by workers in their accounting practices. True, women admitted to this place each achieved the formal label of "battered woman," but inside this residential social service the heterogeneity among women could not be so easily glossed. I turn now to the next type of social problems work: How workers continued to transform the heterogeneity among clients into the homogeneity of the battered woman type of person and in so doing, how workers gave themselves a warrant and a mandate to act toward these women in particular ways.

Chapter Five

Transforming Clients

> The interpretive scheme . . . automatically begins to operate as soon as the inmate enters, the staff having the notion that entrance is *prima facie* evidence that one must be the kind of person the institution was set up to handle.
>
> Erving Goffman, *Asylums*

In most constructions, shelter clients are known only as each is an instance of the "battered woman," a homogeneous collective representation, a type of woman with a particular set of personal characteristics, experiences, subjectivities, problems, and needs. Against this assumption of client homogeneity stands the heterogeneity of actual shelter clients.

True, South Coast worker selection practices were oriented to selecting clients who were instances of the battered woman type of person and true, worker rhetorical practices transformed heterogeneity into homogeneity—on-the-record. Yet, given the heterogeneity of lived realities, we would not logically anticipate that individual clients would define themselves and their experiences in any one way or that observers would see each and every shelter client as a classic exemplar of the battered woman.

This logical prediction of client heterogeneity was magnified by selection characteristics and procedures at South Coast. For example, workers could cite many instances where service petitioners had, quite understandably, consciously manipulated impressions in order to secure entry to scarce housing; an "emergency" or a referral from another shelter could override all other impressions; expectations were relaxed on days when there was plenty of space and so on. Further and critically, workers and clients did not always agree that a new client *was* an instance of a battered woman. Upon entry, for example, one woman said her husband was "just ill" while the admitting worker argued that he was a "classic batterer"; according to a worker at another time, one client "wasn't aware of it but she had been raped"; a note for another new client said this woman refused to label herself as "a battered woman" because "she has a very strong stereotype of what a battered woman is and she does not want to fit that stereotype." Still another client told me her husband was not a batterer. According to her, "he just needs me away from him to get his head together."

In brief, even though workers *never asked* a woman how she defined herself, there were numerous indications anyway that not all women selected for South Coast agreed with workers that each was an instance of the battered woman. Still further, it would be difficult to support the construction of shelter clients as women who chose to leave their homes. Workers noted that several new clients were assaulted but had requested entry only after they had been kicked out of their homes;[1] a few clients apparently entered at the strong urging of local social service providers;[2] a few others were somewhat forcibly removed from their homes by police.[3] For many reasons, then, it would be illogical to assume that each and every woman achieving South Coast entry saw herself or was easily seeable by all others as a classic exemplar of the battered woman type of person.

Despite client heterogeneity, South Coast, like other such places, had a homogeneous service goal—to help clients become independent and self-sufficient. In social problem claims, this often sounds like an automatic process: The battered woman enters a shelter; she lives with other such women, gets support, and then she leaves "not the same person." But such a claim is problematic on two counts. First, it disguises the social problems work arising from the fact of client heterogeneity and the fact of service goal homogeneity. Despite heterogeneity, workers had to construct individual clients as instances of the type of woman for whom the organization existed. This would be a necessary activity for without it work would be meaningless, since all efforts were justified only for this particular type of woman. Second, claims that shelter clients are automatically transformed disguises the actual work of such places, the social problems work of transforming a battered woman type of person into an antithetical type of person—a strong and independent woman.

This is my topic. I want to further examine how workers used the battered woman collective representation as an interpretive device to make sense of clients. This time I am interested in how they used this device to justify their practical activities of "supporting" identity change. Since the general interpretive scheme and the structural arrangements at South Coast allowed—and encouraged—workers to intervene into clients' lives in particular ways, I will begin there.

Interpretive schemes, organizational structure, and identity transformation

> This is a shelter that has a program. The shelter can't be all things to all people.
>
> Family Violence Program Administrator

Organizational rhetoric, constructing clients as unique individuals who should engage in self-determination, was bounded first by the battered woman collective representation serving as an interpretive device to make sense of individual clients. This device was—and still is—in the cultural scene; it is visible in magazine articles, television talk shows, and in movies about the battered woman; this device was explicitly taught to workers in their weekly training sessions.

In their talk, workers constructed the battered woman client as a unique type of person. One day, for example, they complained to me about their training: "All our training has been about battered women. We need training about women-in-transition, too." Such a comment, of course, is sensible only if these two client types were different. On another day, a worker complained about organizational rules when she said, "Our rules don't fit women-in-transition." This is a sensible comment only given the assumption that rules *did* make sense for the battered woman client. And, an entry in the shelter log about one new client said: "Her needs are the same as other residents. She needs to become independent and increase her self-esteem." This comment is sensible only given assumptions that all clients were the same and that all needed to become independent and increase their self-esteem. In brief, workers constructed the battered woman as a unique type of person. At South Coast, there were three general aspects to workers' construction of this type of person.

First, similar to social problems claims, workers constructed "wife abuse" as a very dangerous activity. They always gave priority entry to service petitioners judged to be in need of housing because of extreme danger, and once inside the shelter, workers remain oriented to clients as women in situations of *continuing* danger. Constructing the battered woman in this way furnished a primary justification for fostering her identity change: It was *necessary* for her physical safety.

Second and also similar to social problems claims, workers constructed "wife abuse" as an unstoppable activity where assailants only "appear" to change. This understanding added another justification to the necessity of fostering identity change in clients: There was *no choice* because the violence and danger would not somehow magically disappear.[4]

Third, although I will discuss in the next chapter how workers did modify their understandings of the characteristics of the battered woman type of person, they nonetheless maintained the major construction that a constellation of victims' personal characteristics (economic, legal and emotional dependence, traditional understandings of gender and family, low self-esteem, accepting blame for the violence, etc.) kept women trapped within violence. Given the service goal of transforming such a woman into a strong and independent woman, this construction can be read as a listing of what must be changed. If the goal of shelter work is to be realized, *these characteristics* must be changed.

In summary, as with any collective representation, the battered woman collective representation is open-ended, the characteristics of this type of person cannot be fully enumerated. My point here is simply that South Coast workers were oriented to clients as they were a particular type of person with a particular set of characteristics requiring a particular type of transformation. According to this logic—which is the logic of claims constructing the battered woman type of person—a good shelter worker, despite competing rhetoric emphasizing client self-determination, would actively and self-consciously attempt to change those characteristics associated with women's entrapment and physical danger.

Organizational rhetoric constructing clients as unique individuals who should engage in self-determination also was bounded by the organizational structure. First and most obvious, there were the services offered by workers. Advocacy was the practical effort to secure clients the services they needed to obtain identity transformation. Workers here assisted clients in obtaining expert help for resolving subjective entrapments blocking independence (counseling), in gaining the material means to self-sufficiency (housing, welfare, jobs), to legal independence (divorce and child custody), to punish offenders (prosecution), and to protect women from further assault (restraining orders). Although each client did not require each service, it remains that the advocacy in which workers specialized was deemed a priori relevant for the battered woman type of person. Hence, workers did *not* develop resources to help clients reconcile with their partners; they had strong links with persons prosecuting abusers but none with those who defended such men; they referred clients only to two counselors, both of whom specialized in counseling the battered woman.

Just as services were oriented to the particular needs of a particular type of person, so, too, were organizational rules. Workers deemed some rules as necessary for the battered woman who is a woman in a situation of continuing danger (three day minimum stay, no contact with outsiders for three days, permission to remain away), as necessary for a woman who needs to get in touch with her feelings (support group attendance, no alcohol or drugs), as necessary for a woman who needs to belong to a community of women (participation in shelter life).[5]

There was one other informal rule at this place. It was written nowhere but agreed upon by all workers: Women must remain focused on "why they are at this place." This was a rule about talk. Inside South Coast there were only three approved topics of conversation: How bad life had been with the partner, how good life would be without him, and how to achieve this better life. Of course, when clients talked among themselves they would cover a range of topics; they would talk positively about aspects of their past lives, and about their aspirations for reconciliation with their partners. But when a worker entered the room such talk would stop. At one time this disjuncture became a real problem when clients petitioned workers to allow them to talk about "something other than our problems." Workers held firm. South Coast was a place for women to achieve independence, doing so required that they remain focused on why they were there, and what they must do to achieve the goal of independence.

Myriad rules at South Coast each were justified by workers' constructions of the battered woman type of person. Each rule also is sensible within sociological understandings of the process of identity transformation. According to Peter Berger and Thomas Luckmann, identity transformation requires that a person who is to be transformed must be isolated from others who might reconfirm the old identity; it requires a new "plausibility structure" to replace the old ways of making sense of the self and experience; it requires a strong affective identification with persons representing the new identity.[6] Workers did not speak in such terms. What they accumulated was practical experience of what was and was not good for clients who needed to establish new identities. From their experience, they learned it was most likely for a client to return to her partner within the first three days of South Coast residence, if she had made no friends at this place, if she had just spent time with her old friends, family or partner. Sociological understandings of the process of identity transformation, in other words, were confirmed by worker practical experience. According to workers, this was a place for the battered woman and each rule was justifiable as necessary for this type of person. What a priori was good for her was her transformation from a battered woman to a strong and independent woman.[7]

The organizational and rhetorical stage now is set for examining the social problems work of transforming client heterogeneity into the homogeneity of the battered woman and of justifying efforts to transform this type of woman into a strong and independent woman. It would be very convenient for me if these aspects of shelter work were analytically distinguishable, if I could first illustrate how workers transformed heterogeneity into homogeneity, and then show how they justified their work of "supporting" identity transformation. My data are not all that obvious for the practical reason that workers did not make sense of their activities in these terms. They were simply making sense of clients and they justified their activities simply as ways to help clients do what had to be done. Since I must transport an analytic framework into practical experience, my data often will illustrate both minor points as well as the major lesson: Clients with heterogeneous experiences, problems, subjectivities, and needs were constructed on-the-record as a particular type of person and this construction justified worker practical actions oriented toward transforming clients into a different type of person. I shall begin with two general and underlying themes in this social problems work:

Constructing clients as instances of the "battered woman" and the meaning of "support" as used by these workers.

Constructing the battered woman

> There's some clear characteristics about a battered woman. . . .
> He doesn't let her work or have a car and he cuts off ties to fam-
> ily. He doesn't let her get an education or if she's got one she
> can't use it. She admires the man, and she's really scared of
> him, scared to say anything, scared not to say anything.
>
> > Lecture to workers during training session

Recall that part of the task of client selection at South Coast was the
complex process of transforming petitioners' stories into those of a "battered woman" or a "not-battered woman." Although entry to this place
officially constituted a client as a battered woman, workers continued to
construct clients after they were admitted. In *form*, these constructions
were similar to those surrounding shelter entry: They each made sense
of individual clients in terms of the battered woman collective representation. In *content* these constructions of clients often differed from those
justifying entry. While successful petitioners often were constructed as
women in the particular *situation* known as "wife abuse," constructions
of clients often focused on the *subjectivity* associated with the battered
woman type of person. Thus:

> Spent all night talking to Sally, the verbal abuse has taken its toll on
> her, she feels very low self-esteem.
>
> [519]

Or:

> Beth is very upset . . . absolutely no self-esteem, husband treated her
> like a child but she is still in love with him. She feels very helpless
> and lonely.
>
> [328]

Other notes reported on meetings where workers constructed *all*
clients as women sharing similar characteristics arising from similar
experiences:

> Held house meeting, it went wonderfully—women shared feelings
> of frustration and low self-esteem that accompanies being battered.
>
> [358]

Or:

> At meeting, women shared their feelings about feeling inadequate
> and being brainwashed.
>
> [478]

Typical of all log entries, readers are not told the grounds for such worker constructions of shelter clients. Furthermore, readers are not told which of the constructions were made by workers and which were offered by clients on their own behalf. That is, did all clients at one meeting actually say, "I feel inadequate and brainwashed," or was this a worker construction? Did Beth actually say, "I have absolutely no self-esteem," or was this a worker construction of this woman? Did Sally construct herself as having "very low self-esteem?" Did she construct this as a result of her verbal abuse or were these worker constructions of her? From time to time, a note would appear in the log alerting others that a specific client had complained about workers making such constructions,[8] but such notes were rare for the simple reason that within this place questions about the source of constructions were not pertaining to workers who used the log for their own purposes. If clients offered alternative definitions of themselves perhaps it was only because these women had been "brainwashed."

As instances of the battered woman type of person, clients also were routinely constructed as persons needing to transform their emotions, or, in the words of workers, as women needing to "get in touch with their feelings." Similar to social problems claims constructing the battered woman collective representation, workers believed such women were prone to "denial" or "ambivalence," and that such emotions should be transformed to those properly expected of a woman who had been repeatedly and viciously assaulted: anger and sadness.[9] Thus, a worker could construct a client as a woman *needing* such emotions work:

> Madge went up to her room early . . . she needs heavy duty counsel-
> ing and even sooner with anyone who feels they can get her crying
> and angry.
>
> [406]

Or, workers could construct their activities as those of directly instruct-
ing clients in how to label their emotional state:

> Talked to Pat about her calm practical demeanor and her quite
> strong turbulent emotions.
>
> [469]

Or, they could make such preferred emotions a topic of house meetings:

> I had a meeting with the women. . . . We had some discussion of
> being in control and taking responsibility for one's feelings.
>
> [426]

Indeed, workers could even make a game of this emotions work:

> Wanda received a call from [her husband]. She was very upset. . . .
> She was trembling and crying a bit. I had her do an anger release. I
> made up a piece of paper with his name on it and she scribbled it
> out, and I wrote it again in a different way, with hearts, or blue or
> bold. She got into scratching it out and so did [her daughter].
>
> [366]

Of course, a careful reader might well note that all such constructions of clients as instances of the battered woman type of person constructed women as somewhat less than adequate adults—they were constructed as women who were out of touch with their own feelings, as
women who were helpless, frustrated, inadequate, and brainwashed.
True, and this tendency is predictable. South Coast was a service organization, anything about clients that was not pertaining to shelter
work—as defined within the battered woman collective representation—was irrelevant. Shelter records, like those of any social service
agency, did not pretend to contain full, complete, or flattering portraits of
clients. On the contrary, records in such places are ways for workers to
alert one another about problems to be corrected in order for transformation to be successful. In constructing clients as instances of the battered
woman type of person, workers constructed them as women needing
particular types of services for particular types of personal change.

Since *all* log entries in effect constructed clients, I shall move from
this general argument that workers' constructions of clients continued
once women were admitted to this place, to another underlying theme.

Shelters in general and South Coast in particular offer the services of housing and support. What *is* support?

Supporting the battered woman

> She really needs help and support to not go back to her boyfriend who beats her. . . . It seems she has been dependent on men who beat her all her life.
>
> [790]

Workers at South Coast understood their activities as "helping" or "supporting" clients. My question here is: What constitutes support? One answer to this question is found by examining the kinds of activities workers did *not* label as "support."

The battered woman collective representation underlying South Coast focused attention on the *particular* problems and needs of women experiencing the condition called "wife abuse." Such an organizational focus served to define as not-pertaining, or only marginally pertaining, many actual activities of workers. For example, South Coast was a residence and as such clients and their children fell ill and needed to be cared for, there was constant cleaning, cooking, and laundry, and clients often needed transportation assistance. Although much of the work in this place would fall into a category of housework, workers did not label this part of their jobs as "support." Furthermore, workers spent much of their time on the most mundane activities needed to help clients move from their former living situations into new ones: They drove around town finding boxes so that clients could pack their belongings and move from their former homes; they helped clients file change of address forms; they read newspapers and called about apartments and used furniture. Yet these activities also were not labeled as "support." In brief, household labor and the mundane labor of changing residence occupied a large portion of worker time but this was dirty work—necessary but not all that important because this was an organization attempting to resolve the *special* problems of the battered woman type of person.

Within South Coast, the term "support" was used to define those activities needed to transform the identity of the battered woman type of person. Such transformation was twofold; it was about objective and subjective change. Hence, the tension: Shelter residence was limited to thirty days, so should objective or subjective transformation take precedence? This tension was ever present and is perhaps best illustrated by a conversation I overheard one day:

> Worker: You need to get your head together.
> Client: I need to get another job.
> Worker: You need to get your head together before you can do these other things.
> Client: I can't get my head together when I don't have enough money to buy food for myself and my child.

In that instance, the worker explicitly was arguing that subjective transformation ("get your head together") should take precedence over objective transformation ("another job"). Granted, workers could argue that objective transformation was difficult yet in practice, they often disagreed with clients when clients wanted to focus on objective transformation. These workers could justify their general tendency to worry the most about perceived needs for subjective transformation.[10] After all, according to one worker:

> We have to focus on why she's at the shelter. If we get right into the nitty gritty of this and say, "now you have to get a place to live and child care and AFDC and all that," we just contribute to her minimizing and denying what happened. When all the concrete things are so difficult to deal with, it's somehow easier as an option for her to return to that situation because we've disregarded the violence.

Thus, South Coast workers most often were first and foremost oriented to changing clients' *subjective* identities. This was the primary goal of support, and, according to one worker, this was logical:

> You've got thirty days in the shelter, thirty days to do a lot of stuff, but what we're really talking about is that the root purpose of the shelter is to change women's identity.[11]

As a consequence, the label, "support," most often was used to note when workers had attempted subjective identity transformation or when further worker efforts at such transformation were justifiable. To give only a few examples, support was justified when a client was constructed as a woman not aware of her own needs:

> Dorothy and I had a long talk. She hasn't told her boyfriend any-
> thing about exactly why she left and where she is!! When she talks
> with him, she gets absorbed in his wants, etc. and totally forgets her-
> self. She really needs constant support.
>
> [430]

Likewise, support was made justifiable by constructing a client as a
woman who had reconfirmed her old identity:

> Kathy is trying to contact her husband. She will require lots of sup-
> port this evening.
>
> [693]

Or, it was justifiable when a client was constructed as a woman who was
trying to discard her old identity:

> Rose came back and we talked for a long while about [her husband].
> She's trying to make a break from him. I feel we really need to sup-
> port her in this.
>
> [642]

Or, support was made justifiable by constructing a woman as having a
difficult time shedding this old identity:

> Delores back from visit with husband. She expressed worry that she
> may return. We need to support her.
>
> [577]

Stated simply, as used at South Coast, "support" was the prescription for any perceived characteristic or experience deemed to be interfering with identity transformation. I shall now repeat a familiar but important story: Readers of the log are neither told anything about the process
of interaction surrounding these entries, nor the grounds for such worker
constructions and prognosis. We do not know which—if any—of these
clients said to workers, "I want support." But once again, this would not
matter much among workers. Regardless of whether or not an independent observer or the client herself would agree with workers' constructions, it remained that once individual clients were constructed as
instances of the battered woman type of person a constellation of prob-

lems and needs followed. Given that clients each were instances of this type of person then identity transformation was necessary, given that identity transformation was necessary then anything interfering with it was a problem to be resolved—something requiring support.

But what did workers *do*? Again, I remind my readers that since workers themselves saw all of their activities as simply those of "supporting clients," my data do not fall into clear categories.

The activities of support

> This place is not just to get you out of a violent situation, but to give you strength. You can make it, you can stand on your feet and make it by yourself. We've been taught before that we need a male, but this is the place where you find out how you don't need a male.
>
> Worker to clients in a support group

In sociological terms, although not in worker terms, the first task of identity transformation would be segregating clients from persons likely to reconfirm old identities. Workers could, for example, enforce the rule prohibiting a new client from contacting anyone within the first three days of her shelter stay:

> Debra wanted to call her boyfriend. I told her no. She was on the 72-hour hold. I told her we don't contact the batterer and that she could call him in three days.[12]

[424]

In this instance, if the worker really did say to this woman "we do not contact the batterer," then more than segregation was accomplished. The client wanted to call her boyfriend. The worker relabeled him as the "batterer," certainly a label discouraging further contact with him.[13]

Workers also could segregate clients from others likely to reconfirm old identities by using their power over the telephone. Their informal power to suspend telephone privileges could be justified, for example, by constructing a woman as not strong enough to resist pressures to return to her old identity:

> Jill has been talking with [her husband] for about an hour. I feel Jill

can be swayed easily. I told her she has five more minutes on the phone.

[420]

At other times, workers could intercept calls and issue direct instructions to outsiders:

Susan's friend called to tell Susan that Susan's husband has been calling in an attempt to reach her. I told her to tell him to leave her alone.

[585]

Or, they could instruct one another to block calls to specific clients:

Sharon back. [Her husband] called twice while she was out. It's real important that she doesn't talk to him.

[618]

These last two examples are intriguing because workers did not offer an explicit justification for their activities and furthermore, readers of the log do not know whether or not it was the worker or a client making the decision for the action. That is, we do not know whether *Susan* said, "Tell my friend to tell my husband to leave me alone." We do not know whether *Sharon* said, "It's real important I don't talk to him." But no matter. Once clients were constructed as instances of the battered woman type of person their segregation was justifiable.

So, workers could segregate clients but this was not enough to dismantle old identities. After all, South Coast had neither bars at the windows nor guards at the doors; clients were "free" to terminate their residence at any time.[14] Furthermore, after the first three days, clients could come and go as they pleased during the day and evening hours, phone calls could not always be monitored. Since clients could therefore be receiving ongoing reconfirmations of their old identities, workers were faced with the task of convincing clients that these old identities were dispreferred.

While the underlying theme of worker activities was to "support" clients in recognizing and getting in touch with emotions properly associated with the battered women type of person, the actual conversations between workers and clients often centered on offering clients new ways to think about their old identities. Given workers' concerns about clients' safety and given their belief that wife abuse is unstoppable, many of these conversations centered on teaching clients how to construct their former partners as "dangerous persons." The following note, for example, described an apparent reality-definition contest between a client who constructed her partner as a "sympathetic character" and a worker who constructed this man as a "dangerous person":

> Jane's boyfriend is extremely dangerous and Jane doesn't want to do anything about him. She feels sorry for him and doesn't want to put him in jail. I impressed the fact on her that he is very dangerous and could kill her.
>
> [601]

Apparently, this worker-defined "fact" of danger could be directly conveyed to a client:

> Talked with Peg. Brought to her attention how very dangerous her ex-boyfriend is.
>
> [466]

As a specific activity of support, workers attempted to teach clients how to construct their partners' violence—certainly a plausibility structure promoting a definition of the old identity as dangerous and in need of transformation. In the same way, although not particularly common, workers could directly instruct a client's *partner* in how to construct *his* behavior:

> Mary's husband . . . tried to deny hitting her, in essence, by saying she had no scars!!!! I said she didn't have to have scars and the marriage vows didn't give him permission to hurt her in any manner.
>
> [357]

Likewise, workers could tell clients how to construct their partners' *present* behaviors in ways typifying such a man as one not likely to change his old, oppressive ways:

> Talked with Tina for quite a while. Her husband is being really nice to her—offering to pay deposit and first month rent on an apartment; also will help her look for a place and will pay for food for first

month. I am suspicious—wonder why he is being so nice (a manip-
ulative move on his part to keep a hold on her for the future?) I told
Tina my feelings and asked her to think about it more.

[359]

For this work of supporting clients in throwing off their old identities,
workers could have assistance. Given the communal living arrangement
and the lack of privacy, other clients could sometimes diagnose characteristics preventing another client from throwing off an old identity:

Tami expressed the desire to have a meeting tomorrow to talk with
Sara. She feels Sara is not facing dealing with her problems. Tami
wants to confront her with this and support her.

[405]

But most commonly, workers found help from other social service per-
sonnel in the local community. Workers at South Coast, for example,
could relay to their clients the constructions of these area professionals:

I told her about her boyfriend's not meeting with [counselor] who
said she should not return home as yet.

[599]

At other times, South Coast workers could consult these area professionals:

Greta called her husband. He received the restraining order today.
He told her that he will be going to [another town]. I fear he may be
setting her up in some kind of trap . . . I think [District Attorney's
office] should be called about this for another opinion on the matter.

[334]

The construction of clients, in brief, could involve South Coast
workers and those in other social service agencies in a circle going
around and around:

Amy said her psychologist talked to her husband's psychologist and
her psychologist feels Amy should leave the area. The feeling is that
Amy's husband is unstable and could be dangerous to her, and that
Amy might not be strong enough to stay away from him.

[400]

On one hand, these entries most certainly raise questions about client confidentiality within South Coast. Workers here regularly exchanged information given to them in confidence; they regularly conspired to ensure that individual clients received the "same story" in their rounds of contacting various social service agencies. Yet workers rarely talked of these activities as morally problematic. After all and by definition, clients were instances of the battered woman, a woman in dire need of identity transformation. If others could "support" South Coast workers in their "support" of clients, then all the better.

Support therefore was the work of enforcing clients' segregation from those apt to confirm old identities; it was the process of giving clients new ways to think about old identities; it was the work of gathering assistance from other clients and from area professionals who seemingly spoke with more authority than did these nonprofessional South Coast workers. Yet, it was not enough to support clients' dismantling of old identities, the old identity had to be replaced by a *new* one:

> Becky and Jane . . . are both considering returning to the men who beat them. Spend as much time with them as possible; help them to identify with other women and encourage them to participate in shelter activities.
>
> [619]

Through enforcing informal rules mandating participation in shelter life, workers could ensure that clients at least had opportunities to develop affective ties with other women. Through enforcing rules about participation in support groups, workers could ensure that clients at least had access to new plausibility structures supporting identity transformation. But primarily, the activity of supporting client's newly developing identities was accomplished through *talk*:[15]

> Helen came into the office wanting to talk. I lent her my full support as she cried. Her confidence and self-esteem are very low. She really bought her husband's script that she is the most worthless nothing in life. I told her I respected her a great deal for leaving the situation and that bottom line she has strength.
>
> [342]

Within such a construction, of course, worker support for this client's newly developing identity was only sensible. Constructed as a battered woman type of person, Helen was a person who *needed* to cry, a person who *deserved* respect, and a woman who could and definitely should leave the situation she came from.

So, primarily through talk, workers supported clients in the task of constructing new subjective identities. Granted, this process was often associated with considerable emotional turmoil:

> Went back to living room to see how Jamie was. She said she felt better, that it was difficult to get used to the idea that she doesn't have a husband. I supported her and encouraged her. She seems to be breaking through a lot these days. I said crying was good and all part of the healing process.
>
> [346]

According to worker constructions, the process of "breaking through" emotions, the process of accepting the definition of the old identity as bad, and the process of forming a new identity simply was what *had to be done*. Certainly this was a difficult task, yet within South Coast, a client's need for subjective identity transformation was simply taken for granted. Workers supported clients who, they assumed, shared these understandings:

> Tori came down, couldn't sleep. We talked about [her husband] and court today. She was tearful and I told her it's hard to go through seeing him in court especially since she still cares for him, that leaving under this circumstance is especially hard but *she is doing what she has to do and she knows it.* (emphases added)
>
> [407]

This was the form and substance of shelter work at South Coast: Workers constructed individual women as instances of the battered woman type of person and this construction justified workers' practical activities. In brief, shelter work was about "supporting" identity transformation; it was work defined as necessary and good for the battered woman.

Summary

> . . . understanding of what the trouble is and how to cope may be critically shaped by the views and analyses provided

by . . . third parties . . . when an outside party moves from giving advice to active intervention the structure of the trouble
undergoes significant change.

Robert Emerson and Sheldon Messenger,
"The Micro-Politics of Trouble"

The battered woman collective representation continued to be used
by workers as an interpretive device once clients entered South Coast. It
was a worker resource, allowing them to make sense of clients, allowing
them to justify practical actions toward clients. Again, this is supremely
sensible. Just as it made perfect sense to allow instances of the battered
woman to enter this shelter, it made perfect sense to act toward these
women in uniform, predictable ways once they gained entrance. The
stage was set by the organization of South Coast; the sense making for
this scene was provided by the battered woman collective representation,
which informed the organization in the first place.

At this point, some readers might feel anger toward these workers.
What gave them the right to tell clients what they should do? What gave
them the right to suspend client confidentiality, to monitor activities, to
impute emotions and motives? Wasn't this place supposed to be gov-
erned by the ideal of client "self-determination?" Indeed, my analysis of
workers' behaviors as seen through their accounting practices does portray them as meddling. So it was and so it *had to be*. First, these workers
had a job—they were to transform the identities of clients. This is what
they were doing, or at least what they said they were doing. Second,
expecting these workers to do other than what they did would be asking
them to be immoral. Workers understood themselves as helping clients
do what they *had to do* and there was a moral rightness to their position.
I can demonstrate this with a personal experience. One day a client
opened a conversation by telling me about the violence she had experienced. She spoke graphically and at length. Her story was truly horren-
dous and was most certainly the story of a "battered woman." Even if I
had known nothing of the battered woman type of person I would have
feared for her safety. I felt much sympathy and alarm. But then she
changed her tone and proceeded to tell me that she was planning to
return to her partner. At that particular moment I became unconcerned
with the data I was collecting. Without cognitive reflection, it was clear

that I could *not* allow her to continue speaking glowingly about her partner; without cognitive reflection, it was clear that I could not merely sit
and nod my head in agreement. Without cognitive reflection, I did what
any good shelter worker would do: I offered her *support*, meaning I
reminded her of the brutalities she had just told me about, and I
reminded her that she had said her partner had promised to change many
times before.

My reactions to this personal experience are now critical data to me.
From the outside, South Coast workers appear to be just one more
instance of social service workers who interfere in the lives of their
clients without concern for their clients' lived realities. But from the
inside, the behaviors are only logical, and, the behaviors are encouraged
by the structure of the organization. That is, South Coast workers and
clients did not talk about what had been good about a client's former
life, they did not discuss any good points about clients' partners. Inside
South Coast, the women were known only as they were instances of the
"battered woman"; their partners were known only as instances of the
"batterer."[16] Of course this was so. This was an organization with a mission and that mission definitely was not to send women back to whatever had driven them to the shelter in the first place. Day after day all
workers heard about—all they would allow clients to talk about—was
violence and brutality. So, the woman I spoke with had indeed told me
about one part of her life, but she had not told me everything about herself or her partner. My reaction was based on my information, which
was limited, a limitation encouraged by the organization.

In some ways, what we have here is not particular to South Coast or
to other shelters. It is an example of a characteristic of most—if not
all—formally organized social services. As argued by Michael Lipsky,
social service providers do not and cannot know their clients as whole,
unique individuals.[17] Clients can be known primarily as they are
instances of the type of person for whom the organization exists. All
organizational structure and interpretations at South Coast combined to
make a woman's status as a battered woman her most relevant characteristic. Given this, workers' behaviors and interpretations were only logical.

While this is endemic to all social services, the case of South Coast
and other feminist identified shelters raise particular issues, since such

places simultaneously promote a homogeneous service goal—helping clients become independent—while they promote philosophies stressing clients' rights to self-determination. The first issue raised is moral: Is self-determination promoted when a client is engaging in self-destruction? It seems clients' rights to self-determination stopped when *workers believed* their courses of action were self-destructive. Second, it seems that social service ideals of client self-determination can be put into practice when, and only when, clients agree with the organizational image of the problem and the resolution. I would argue that workers at South Coast became directive, that they *had* to become directive because the real world did not produce only classic exemplars of the battered woman type of person. In other words, although social problem claims-makers assumed victimized women would quickly learn to identify themselves as instances of the "battered woman," while they assumed the process would be automatic within shelters, while they assumed victimized women would want to achieve independence, not all shelter clients shared these visions and goals. Hence, the assumed automatic process became tasks for workers to accomplish. When stated this way, I would argue that, on a case by case basis, these workers transformed the heterogeneity of real victimized women into the homogeneity of the "battered woman." This was the social problems work of fitting the heterogeneity of lived realities into the homogeneity of a collective representation.

But this is only one part of the story and only one type of social problems work with clients in social service agencies. Indeed, if taken alone, this discussion would be very misleading because it would give the impression that these workers were able to make sense of all clients in terms of one collective representation. This, in turn, would lead to the impression that workers were organizational robots blindly applying an abstract interpretive scheme to practical experience. Not true, of course.

Most certainly, South Coast workers could and did construct clients as instances of a type of person, and they saw themselves as doing much on behalf of such a woman. But client heterogeneity did not disappear with such rhetorical constructions. So, I will turn to the final questions: How did workers make sense of clients who seemed demanding, troublesome, and somewhat less than grateful? How did they make sense of regularly occurring interpersonal troubles among clients and between themselves and clients? How did they make sense of what objectively could be seen as an overwhelming presence of service failure in reconstituting clients' lives? This is the social problems work of repairing disjunctures between representations and experience; it is the final link completing the reflexive circle of social problems claims, commonsense interpretive devices, and practical experience.

Chapter Six

Making Sense of Shelter Work

One aspect of social problems work . . . involves persons' ongoing maintenance and "repair" of collective representations and
their related complementary oppositions while also explaining
and justifying preferred orientations to issues of practical concern.

> Gale Miller and James Holstein,
> "On the Sociology of Social Problems"

The social problems work of transforming clients into instances of
the battered woman type of person was a way for workers to justify their
interventions into clients' lives and hence, a way for them to make sense
of the *practice* of shelter work. But this work also was an *experience*.
Most certainly, it was the emotional experience of constant talk about
violence; it was the experience of hearing clients' detailed and devastat-
ing stories of their past lives—shelter work was the experience of constant horror.[1] This would be expected given the construction of the battered woman and given that such talk was encouraged by workers. Here,
though, I am concerned with another experience, the experience of per-
ceiving differences between expectations about clients and the realities
of working with clients.

I will begin by reminding my readers of the links between the collective representation of the battered woman type of person and the
organization and operation of shelters. In particular, we would *assume*
that a battered woman somewhat automatically would become a good
member of the shelter community of women; we would *assume* that the
basis of strong interpersonal sentiment and support among clients would
exist due to shared experiences, biographies, subjectivities, and motiva-

tions of a single type of person; we would *assume* that workers' jobs would be those of offering support; we would *assume* a considerable amount of service success given that the shelter organization offers precisely what their clients want and need.

To be clear, such an idealized image could sometimes describe life inside South Coast. My field notes contain many descriptions of impromptu birthday parties for children or clients, of communal dinners where each client pooled her meager food resources to create something special, of clients who became mutually supportive friends, of clients who left this place and went on to live apparently happy and productive independent lives. The model of shelter work at South Coast sometimes did work and this story has been written by others.[2] But my interest here is in the underside of this place—the troubles, the disjunctures between idealized expectations and practical experience. While such troubles have been noted in other shelters,[3] my specific goal here is to examine how workers could reconcile these differences in order to make their work sensible and meaningful. I shall begin by briefly illustrating some types of common troubles within South Coast.

Troubles and disappointments

> Donna talked about her feelings of alienation when women talked about their children because she doesn't have any. Tami doesn't like Lorraine talking about going back to her husband; it makes Tami feel bad since she's leaving her spouse. Tami also told me that Olga is upset because Dora is not cleaning her side of the room. Olga doesn't want to confront Dora herself so someone please make a room check.
>
> [378]

With the exception of notes in the shelter log justifying intake decisions, the log contained more references to interpersonal troubles than to anything else. This is sensible given the formal purpose of this document to alert others about what to expect on upcoming shifts—trouble often reverberated throughout this place. Although workers themselves only noted but did not "categorize" troubles, I will impose an arbitrary classification on some of these log entries and on some of my field notes in order to briefly illustrate the types of disjunctures between expectations and experiences that were part and parcel of the experience of work at South Coast. I will not empirically develop this discussion because my purpose here is only to offer evidence of recurring troubles not only requiring worker sensemaking, but also requiring workers to reconcile the content of the collective representation of the battered woman type of person with their actual experiences with shelter clients.

First, shelters begin operation assuming clients will become good members of the shelter community of women. This, in turn, assumes any differences among clients will not hinder their interpersonal sentiment, and it assumes clients will share resources and will do the communal work necessary to keep the place open and habitable. While these assumptions are sensible within the constructed representation of the battered woman type of person, they were not always met in practical experience.

To begin, clients at South Coast did not always see their similarities as more important than their differences. From time to time there were racial and ethnic antagonisms among women,[4] but most commonly, problems centered on mundane differences in "personality" and "lifestyle." For example, I attended a support group one evening that disintegrated into hostility. In this group there were four women, only one who identified herself as a "married woman." In the course of talking about their past lives, the married woman interrupted the current speaker and said, "Am I the only married woman here?" She continued by labeling the other women "sinners" and reminded them that cohabitation without marriage is not "biblical." While the on duty worker attempted to teach her the organizationally approved ideas that "each woman makes her own choices" and that "violence doesn't depend on a marriage license," the offended client abruptly left the next day saying that South Coast was not a place for her. Similarly, it was very common for clients to lodge formal complaints about the personalities or demeanors of others:

Kara down at midnight, very concerned. All the women are afraid of Jackie—bad language, violence potential, and shock at her stories.
[367]

And, problems due to life-style differences among women could escalate in the communal living situation which offered little privacy:

> Martha got fed up with her child's fussing and put her in her room crying. Sara and Loni went up and got her; brought her down and wanted to feed her. Their rationale was that they thought it was cruel to have her up there crying because she was hungry. Martha got very upset because she felt people were telling her what to do and interfering with her raising her child. I talked with Martha about it; she was really pissed.
>
> [625]

In brief, shelter clients did not always see their similarities as instances of the battered woman type of person as more important than their differences. Furthermore, while a good commune member is a person who shares resources and who realizes that resources will not always be available for personal use, hostility between clients could result from perceptions of improper sharing:

> Maggie and Beth really got into it. Maggie says Beth was on the phone too long and so somehow Maggie missed out on her dinner date. There were a lot of heavy words thrown around including Beth saying to Maggie, "No wonder the old man beat you around so much." Everything seems to be calmed down now, but something has to be done.
>
> [637]

So, clients did not always learn to share communal resources. Further, clients did not always want to do the work they were expected to do. At South Coast, clients were expected to do their assigned share of the communal housekeeping duties, but women routinely complained that this expectation was unfair:

> Abigail came in the office to tell me that Jane had bathed herself and boys, and Abigail doesn't think it is fair for her to have to clean the bathtub after them.
>
> [587]

Indeed, it was not particularly uncommon for clients to simply *refuse* to do their share of the household labor:

Clara up, reminded her of kitchen duty, said she's tired of cleaning up after others. She and Cheryl started a game of backgammon—suggested chores be done first; it is noon. They were very uninterested. I really believe we have to undertake stronger measures to get some kind of order in this house.

[694]

In summary, the model of shelter work depends on clients focusing on their commonalities; it depends on them being good commune members, and such assumptions were only sometimes met at South Coast. Second, the collective representation of the battered woman gives us an image of a good *client*. We would anticipate such a woman would be undemanding, follow worker suggestions and no doubt express gratitude to those saving her from her dire plight. Yet according to workers, some clients could be very demanding:

Boni told me in a "I'm telling you" voice to wake her at 6:45 A.M. I resented her tone of voice, as if my function is to wake her. I suggested she get an alarm clock and with that, she slammed upstairs!!!

[508]

Just as workers constructed some clients as *demanding*, they constructed others as *ungrateful*. Such a woman, for example, might be constructed as one having little faith in workers' abilities to offer support:

Debbie said she wanted to talk to a "counselor." She did not seem satisfied with me. Oh well. Called office and they are setting it up.

[823]

Other clients were constructed as women with many complaints:

I received a lot of information, mostly negative. It seems she's really having a tough time; feels shelter isn't doing anything for her or others. Has feelings that there is not enough real counseling available for the women; she also was feeling resentful concerning chores because she felt she was always having to pick up others' messes.

[340]

Indeed, at one staff meeting, a worker constructed one client as a woman complaining about *everything*:

She's going to leave because she doesn't like the shelter. She doesn't like the clients; she doesn't like the staff; she doesn't like the counseling; she doesn't like the bed; she doesn't like anything. Like, I went grocery shopping with the shelter money and she got upset because I bought the store brands rather than the good brands. She'll only drink Folger's coffee.

And, to continue, some women were not good clients because they *broke organizational rules.* At South Coast it was not atypical for clients to tell others where the place was located, to violate curfew, to bring weapons or drugs into the place, to become intoxicated. Most certainly, such events were troublesome because workers constructed each rule as good for the battered woman:

> Lonna came into office wanting my support to go see boyfriend to tell him they were through. She said he may get violent but she has a gun and will use it if necessary. Told her of "no weapons" rule; told her to get rid of gun; advised her not to go to pool tourney tonight where he will be. She is angry and frustrated with me.
>
> [743]

Finally, although workers were to support clients in making permanent changes in their lives, not all clients were constructed as women actively trying to lay the foundation for their lives after this place. There were countless incidents of clients refusing to contact area social service agencies, forgetting to show up for appointments arranged for them by workers, refusing to look for jobs or housing, spending their first welfare check on a tape recorder or other luxury when they did not have enough money to move from South Coast. In brief, while the organization originally worried that workers would do "too much" for clients, it was not uncommon for workers to be the only persons trying to lay the foundations for women's future lives.

In summary, workers did not construct all clients as instances of the battered woman type of person, who would be a grateful and undemanding client, and a good member of the shelter community. By illustrating these troubles I want only to make one point: Expectations about clients were not always met. On-the-record and in worker talk, workers could disappoint clients, and clients could disappoint workers.

Such disjunctures between expectations and experiences had many consequences for workers. When clients broke rules, workers could become *rule enforcers*; when clients did not work out interpersonal troubles among themselves, workers could become *dispute mediators*; when clients did not do their share of communal housekeeping duties, workers could become *house cleaners*. Each trouble added to the jobs of workers and each of the ensuing tasks held the status of dirty work—activities having nothing to do with the organizational goal of transforming clients' lives, activities which, in fact, interfered with establishing the preferred "supportive" type relationship. Further and critically, when clients did not act grateful, it was difficult to see the meaning of shelter work.

Despite such troubles, South Coast might have offered workers a positive employment experience if worker activities were associated with a high rate of success. In that case, workers might have been able to say "despite troubles, we are successful." But here, too, there were problems. As in other ongoing shelters, the formal measure of service success at South Coast was the number of clients not returning to their abusive partners. In practice, this measure was very ungratifying.

To begin, of the women completing exit forms when they left South Coast, almost sixty percent did not immediately return to their former partners. While this sounds like a very acceptable rate of service success, it cannot stand alone. First, less than half of all clients completed exit forms. I examined information for 159 women and found there was no information on twelve women who entered South Coast and left immediately saying they would not tolerate the noise, the rules, and/or the deplorable living conditions. Several other women apparently left after being told they could not make phone calls during the first three days or that they needed advance permission to remain away from the shelter for a night. Twelve other women did not complete exit forms when they were evicted by workers—one after she lunged at a worker with a kitchen knife. Twenty-seven others simply disappeared without telling workers they would not be returning; another woman fled when workers diagnosed her as a probable child abuser and alerted Child Protective Services; another would not complete forms and threatened a lawsuit maintaining that workers had not "delivered" what they had "promised" at intake. Clearly, the 60 per-

cent success rate figure is based on somewhat less than a full population of women entering South Coast.[5]

But even for those clients leaving in a regular fashion, the organizational measure of success could be unsatisfying. For example, while it
might be true that many women did not return to their former lives, this
does not mean they went on to live independently. On the contrary,
many women went from South Coast to other temporary housing such
as other shelters or cheap hotels; several moved in with their parents.
And, where a woman went directly upon leaving this place had little
relationship to where she would be a month later. It was very common
for a woman to move to her own apartment but then return to her former
partner a week or a month later. Finally, several women who did not
return to their former partners left South Coast to move in with men they
had started dating while living in the shelter—not situations leading
workers to see real "success." In brief, although this organization formally kept track of service success in terms of the number of women not
returning to their former partners, the lack of information on many
women, further requests for services from women who were initially
"successful," and the ungratifying new living arrangements of many formally successful clients made this measure problematic.

The practical experiences of doing shelter work therefore could challenge the image of this work as honorable, good, and important. For
frontline workers, the job was low pay and involved long hours; the skills
accumulated would not catapult them into future high paying employment. If workers were not repaid for their efforts in terms of client gratitude and deference, if clients were constructed as women who could
resent workers' efforts, if the organizational measure of success was so
unsatisfying—what would be left?[6] Granted, there was rapid worker
turnover and granted, at least some of these workers had no choice but to
stay because they needed a job, but it remains these workers were
able—at times—to neutralize troubles and hence to salvage the meaning
of their work. This is the social problems work of repairing disjunctures
between the expected and the experienced. My examination will have
three parts: How the battered woman collective representation used as an
interpretive device could neutralize troubles, how it failed to neutralize all
troubles, and how it could neutralize objective service failure.

Making sense of interpersonal troubles

> The worst thing is when you get women in here that have to be
> told to take care of their children. They are trying to save
> enough to get out on their own and they go blow all their money
> on something. They have a golden opportunity here and they
> *can't take advantage of it.* (emphases added)
>
> Shelter Worker

Although South Coast workers maintained the primary collective
representation images of the battered woman type of person, they did
modify this representation in one way that allowed them to *categorically*
neutralize *all* interpersonal troubles. Rather than constructing such a
woman as one who will quickly and somewhat automatically overcome
the myriad effects of her victimization once she leaves her home, workers constructed her as a type of woman likely to suffer *long-term* consequences from her victimization. For example, they could link the particular experience of "long-term dependence" with the production of a
woman likely to be a very demanding client:

> Nine out of ten women haven't done anything for themselves in
> their life. They have never had to support themselves; the husband
> has provided. They demand more because they've always had
> someone to care for them. They need 24-hour care.

They also could account for demanding and seemingly ungrateful clients
in terms of the consequences of long-term abuse. Indeed, according to
one worker, this experience could make it impossible to please clients:

> These women have been powerless for so long that when they get
> into the shelter they have to have someone they can blame. They're
> persecuting you because they are powerless. You're in a no-win sit-
> uation; you can't please her.

Alternatively, workers could combine the "ignorance of social services"
characteristic attributed to the battered woman with such a woman's
"dependency" and account for why clients would be unhappy with the
organization:

They come in with the expectation that there is a highly trained clinical staff here and they'll get excellent counseling, a lot of misconceptions. Plus, there are women who often are not used to taking charge. A woman may come in expecting not to have any requirements made of her.

Finally, workers could construct the personal experience of "wife abuse" and the emotional turmoil of "leaving home" in a way combining to make clients into a type of person who was incapable of managing her own affairs:

> . . . you bring anybody into the shelter and you've changed her life and she's gone through fear and getting hit and she doesn't feel good and she's confused. . . . I'm bound to assume she can't do much for herself.

By constructing shelter clients as instances of the battered woman and by constructing this type of person as a woman suffering *continuing* consequences from her victimization, workers could categorically neutralize a range of interpersonal troubles. Within such constructions, clients might be *expected* to be demanding, ungrateful, confused, and ignorant—not because of anything about the organization or its workers, but because of the personal consequences of the condition known as "wife abuse." Thus, all troubles could be neutralized by constructing them as consequences of clients' personal experiences:

> I think that residents will always have gripes, will always periodically think that staff doesn't care about them, that staff isn't working, that staff isn't treating them properly. Sometimes it's because staff don't check chores, sometimes it's because they do check chores. It seems real arbitrary because it's only because of what the client is going through. Not so much what the staff is doing, more about residents' personal situation.

Of course, a critical reader might well note that such worker constructions of their clients are a long way from the formal organizational image of these clients as women who are "strong within themselves." This is true. At the same time, such categorical modifications of the battered woman collective representation do not change the image that such a woman deserves workers' sympathy and support.[7] Indeed, worker modifications *increase* the sympathy margin due such a woman. That is, a battered woman type of person within workers' constructions might indeed act like a troublesome, demanding, confused, and ungrateful client, *but this is not her fault.* Such negative characteristics are the consequences of her victimization, consequences so severe they do not simply disappear the moment she leaves her home.

While workers in their talk could categorically neutralize all interpersonal troubles within South Coast, this was not particularly common. Rather, troubles most often were neutralized by situated accounts. In these instances, a given troublesome client would be constructed as a battered woman and then one or another characteristic of this type of person would be used to neutralize the specific trouble at hand.

This device could be used by workers, for example, to neutralize clients' complaints. In one instance, the following worker description of an apparently tense house meeting implicitly incorporated a client into the battered woman social collectivity by constructing her as an "inherently weak person." In a line of implicit reasoning, the worker transformed an appearance of "hatefulness" into an indication of "emotional confusion," something expected of this type of woman:

> Bonnie was extremely hostile—she feels being at the shelter is taking charity and her daddy never took charity and she wouldn't be here except for the kids. She said some mean things to me. I finally realized that Bonnie has to appear strong and when she feels weak she won't allow herself to feel it so she pushes people away and acts hateful instead.
>
> [431]

At another time, a worker neutralized a new client's complaint about the one-dollar a day suggested rent by constructing this complaint as a consequence of "defensiveness," which was constructed as an indication of "emotional confusion" given the worker perceived fact that the shelter was really "on her side." The complaint thus was neutralized and indeed, it was transformed into a mandate to offer this new client support:

> She's very hostile, indignant when told of rent—she was at another shelter and said they had no charge. I tried to talk to her and

repeated she needn't be defensive here, we're on her side. She needs a lot of support.

[510]

In a variation on the same theme, workers could use this sensemaking to neutralize other troubles within the environment. For example, they could construct troublesome interactions as consequences of the frustration and misplaced anger characterizing the battered woman type of person:

Had a chat with Eleanor. She is very angry and frustrated about not being able to go out and do things on her own without fearing boyfriend will show up. I feel her anger at this situation is being directed to whoever she's talking to.

[756]

In the same way, they could neutralize troubles between clients and their children:

Talked with Sandi who seems depressed about never being able to find housing that allows children. She was taking her anger out on [her child]. I confronted her with it.

[401]

Finally, just as workers could have assistance in their work of supporting clients, workers in other agencies could neutralize trouble by constructing South Coast clients as instances of the battered woman. Once, for example, this was used to neutralize a client's generally troublesome if not bizarre behavior:

When [local counselor] called she said that Louise was not on drugs but she may have brain damage due to battery . . . She felt we should deal with Louise as a woman who has been through some tough beatings.

[795]

In each of these instances, workers neutralized troubles by constructing clients as instances of the battered woman type of person and then using this as an interpretive device to make sense of the woman's behavior. So, Bonnie was constructed as a woman who "acted hateful" *because* she was "really weak"; a new client was constructed as a woman who acted "hostile and indignant" *because* she was "confused and needed support"; Eleanor and Sandi were constructed as women who were "acting hostile" *because* of "misplaced anger"; Louise was constructed as a generally troublesome client *because* she "had been through some tough beatings." In each case, one or another trouble was attributed to an underlying cause—the woman was an instance of the battered woman.

Inside South Coast, this was a powerful resource, allowing workers to make sense of the unexpected and the troublesome. Indeed, this device could do more than merely neutralize troubles—it could construct troubles in a way promoting them as *positive* for the client, a woman defined a priori as one needing to do emotions work. So, for example, a client's complaint about an organizational procedure could be constructed as a "healthy sign":

> I told Liza she may have to move to another room and she was running around ranting and raving about how she had just started to become comfortable in that room!! I said her emotions were starting to come out and it was a healthy sign.
>
> [396]

Or, an apparently tense worker/client interaction could be constructed as one leading a client to "feel a lot better":

> Gloria still bitching constantly. And I strongly reprimanded her. Then I asked her if she felt safe, etc. and I explained the needs of all women here. She was very hostile and irate and then finally broke into tears and cried for about a half hour. A lot of pent-up tension was released and she seems to feel a lot better.
>
> [334]

All these are examples of the social problems work of repairing disjunctures between expectations about the battered woman and worker experiences with women residing at South Coast. In myriad ways, workers could construct trouble as mere consequences of the condition called "wife abuse," and they could construct their disturbing interactions as "good" for clients who needed to get in touch with their emotions.

Again, a critical reader might well note that this rhetoric was very convenient for workers because it allowed them to deflect a range of complaints and problems back on to clients.[8] This is true, but just as clearly, their use of this device was associated with practical advantages for *clients*.

Simply stated, constructing clients as instances of the battered woman justified continuing to offer sympathy and support to clients who seemingly defied the norms of reciprocity in sympathy exchange—when women did not act grateful and when they were not good clients. More concretely, workers justified rule suspension in this way. For example:

> She came back late, smelling of booze. I asked her if she'd been drinking and she said she'd had a beer. She was sobbing hysterically—it was good to see her let out her feelings. She saw her husband and he said to her he didn't want to make their marriage work and is living again with his girlfriend. She is beginning to realize that she can only count on herself and she is best to go ahead and make plans and take responsibility for her own life.
>
> [343]

As usual, readers of the log do not know anything about the process of interaction surrounding this entry. But no matter. On-the-record, this client was forgiven for her rule violations. Indeed, the violations become lost in the sadness of her story, the story of a battered woman. She was constructed as a woman who had violated rules *because* of her emotional upset. Indeed, as constructed, the time she spent away from South Coast had been beneficial because it had led her to "realize" her marriage was over, and it had led her to "let out her feelings." Although the worker could have justifiably evicted this woman for coming back after curfew and for drinking alcohol, no penalty was forthcoming.

Thus, the general rule: Just as it was to a woman's practical advantage to be constructed as a battered woman type of person in order to achieve shelter entry, it was to her advantage to be constructed as such a woman once inside South Coast. What this required, of course, cannot be enumerated: all constructions were situated and folk reasoning lie under them. Regardless of this complexity, it remains that the battered woman collective representation used as an interpretive device could neutralize rule violations just as it could neutralize worker disappointments, something clearly to the advantage of clients who wanted the services offered by this organization.

Therefore it is not surprising that clients could offer constructions of *themselves* as instances of the battered woman. For example, at one time two clients were becoming very troublesome because their interactions with one another were disturbing others. Workers were becoming upset and had started talking among themselves about what "should be done." The following note reported that one of these women constructed herself as an instance of the battered woman type of person and thus neutralized the problem with her behavior:

> Since Debbie and Gayle were pissed at each other, I wanted them to deal with it. . . . Anyway, I was up til 2:30 A.M. having a counseling session with them re: their built-up resentments. It turned out finally that Gayle ended up crying and saying she's been upset about her divorce and taking her feelings out on Debbie.
>
> [376]

At other times, clients constructed themselves as instances of the battered woman type of person to counter workers' interpretations leading to negative sanctions. For example, one client came close to eviction for breaking rules. Yet plans to "do something" about her were put on hold, perhaps because workers accepted the construction she offered of herself as a "battered woman":

> I explained due to her coming in 1 1/2 hours after curfew with booze on her breath that these were the grounds to ask her to leave the shelter. She said she knew nothing of the rules; she said when she saw them she was too emotionally upset.
>
> [462]

Another client countered a worker's interpretation of her as a "drug user" by constructing herself as "tearful:"

> Debbie came in. I asked her if she was high. She said no, her eyes were swollen because she had been crying.
>
> [590]

Indeed, the construction of a client as a battered woman type of person was so powerful that one woman successfully used it to neutralize one of the most problematic incidents ever occurring among South Coast clients. It began one day when a client made a negative, racist remark about the child of this woman. The offended mother grabbed a butcher knife and started to move toward the client making the negative comment. She would not give back the knife and kept waving it; it took several minutes for all the other clients and the on duty worker to get the knife back. Needless to say, the situation was frightening and intolerable. The worker went into the office and started to call another worker to support her decision to immediately evict the knife wielding client. But before this call was made the woman went into the office and apparently excused her behavior as that of a battered woman. She was not evicted and the incident was transformed from one of frightening trouble to one of "education":

> I spent an hour talking to her. She was crying and said the incident reminded her of when her husband used to scream at her and then hit her and she would always be in the kitchen and grab for a knife to protect herself. I told her it was ironic that she was trying to protect her kids from verbal abuse and then she acts in a violent manner. I said I hope she'd talk with her children and let them know that she felt that what she did was wrong and not a good way to handle anger.
>
> [412]

Clearly, neutralizing trouble by constructing a client as an instance of the battered woman type of person was effectively accomplished by both workers and clients. But if I stopped discussion here, it might seem as if this device always was used to make sense of any situation. Not true. This device was merely a *resource*, and one with limitations surrounding its effectiveness.

Practical sensemaking and failures to neutralize troubles

> Paula called, wanted to be out until 2:00 A.M. I said no, that she had better get right back, that we weren't a country club and she knew better. I also told her that she would soon have her own

place and that's the time for her to start dating. It sounded like she was in a bar or nightclub.

[474]

Although constructing a particular client as an instance of the battered woman type of person could be extremely effective in neutralizing troubles, the use of this device by workers was bounded in two ways. First, the application of the device depended on practical sensemaking. As with justifications for selection decisions, folk reasoning underlay construction of clients. In effect, constructing clients' behaviors as those of a battered woman type of person involved a leap of faith—present behaviors had to be understood as consequences of past experiences. Although it is not possible to enumerate the grounds upon which workers decided this leap was or was not sensible, I can give examples of how *failures* to neutralize trouble could be accomplished by constructing a client as a "not-battered woman." For example, in one instance a worker did not neutralize trouble by constructing doubt about whether or not a client's story and emotional demeanor were those of a battered woman type of person:

> Talked with Gladys. She came in because her boyfriend's brother slapped her and her boyfriend yelled at her. She couldn't go to her girlfriend's because they had an argument last night. The problem is her attitude, she doesn't do anything to improve her situation . . . I explained to her my feelings toward her (i.e. pointed out contradictions in her story) and my reaction to her attitude. I got no reaction except for a dirty look. She showed no emotion.
>
> [617]

Or, a failure to neutralize trouble could be accomplished by constructing a client as a woman who was not displaying the expected demeanor of a battered woman type of person:

> We asked her to leave. She would take no responsibility for her behavior—coming in late and drinking. She felt being fifteen minutes late was no big deal. She rationalized her behavior and criticized staff as a means to divert us off her case. We asked her to leave in the morning, she was quite angry.[9]
>
> [463]

Or, a failure to neutralize trouble could be justified by constructing the client as a "not-battered woman" because she was *too* angry. In one instance, this was accomplished even though a possible justification for the client's upset was duly noted:

> Ella became furious after talking with a relative on the phone and began pounding on walls and broke the bulletin board. I told her we would not allow that violent behavior here. She can be angry but not act out that way. She was verbally belligerent to me. We told her we will ask her to leave if she has any more violent outbursts like that.
> [752]

The use of the battered woman collective representation as an interpretive device therefore was bounded by folk reasoning and workers' abilities to accomplish a leap of faith in order to neutralize the present in terms of an imputed past. Second, their use of this device depended on their willingness to forgive. That is, constructing a client as troublesome *because* she was a battered woman simultaneously demanded that she be forgiven. To do otherwise would be to blame her for her troubles, something not allowed at South Coast. Thus, the use of this device was reflexively related to workers' willingness to forgive. In the words of one worker, this could be difficult:

> A lot of these women aren't likable. They've been through too much. But when you're working with these women, they're difficult and you get to the point that you want to punch them yourself.

Or, in the words of another worker, regardless of the underlying reason for the troublesome behavior, it could be "real hard" to ignore the immediate experience:

> You have to maintain a sense of humor and you can't let the women become your enemies, like the clients who rip off the towels and ruin the rooms and all that stuff. Those things are real hard, to look at that woman and say "these are the reasons, she's been socialized and dependent and she's been through a lot." She's a general fuckup and we wouldn't want to live with her either.

In brief, the condition of wife abuse might indeed produce women who are demanding, ungrateful, and generally troublesome. but to use this device was to forgive and these workers were practical actors, not saints. As such, there were limits to their forgiveness, limits on when they would construct a troublesome client as an instance of the battered woman type of person. When behavior was not filtered through this interpretive device worker anger—not forgiveness—was justified:

> Doris wanted us to watch the three kids today. I said, "no." She then asked if we had a volunteer coming in. I said, "no, I was on shift alone." Then she said angrily, "Never mind. I'll take care of it myself." The thing that annoys me is that she EXPECTS us to bend over backward and when we don't she gets pissed.
>
> [539]

In summary, workers' constructions of troublesome behaviors as a consequence of the condition called "wife abuse" depended first on their folk reasoning. On a case by case basis, they decided whether or not this *particular* behavior was so understood. Sure, one troublesome episode could be deflected, but from the workers' perspectives, clients some-times went too far. What if a particular client repeatedly violated rules? What if she did little but complain about the organization and demand workers do things they were incapable of doing? What if she simply refused to do anything to help herself and rather spent her time having fun with her friends? Each of these situations *theoretically* could be understood as behaviors of a battered woman type of person but the kinds of cognitive leaps necessary to bring some actual behaviors into line with expectations—and organizational demands—were sometimes too much for these workers who were practical actors. Second, workers' constructions of troublesome behaviors were bounded by their willing-ness to continue offering sympathy even when a client was treating them poorly or when her behavior was wrecking havoc on the shelter environ-ment. To construct a particular behavior as a consequence of wife abuse was to justify continued sympathy, but certainly this was *reflexive*: The construction of a woman as a "battered woman" demanded she be accorded sympathy but, if workers experienced anger toward a woman, then she would *not* be constructed as a "battered woman." Workers' con-structions of clients, in brief, were inextricably tied both to their folk rea-soning and to their emotional reactions toward these women.

In the end, some women lost their membership in the battered woman social collectivity. In theory and in practice, South Coast was not for them. This was the social problems work of repairing disjunctures between collective images and lived experience. By definition, a "battered woman" *is* a good and grateful client. By definition she *is* a good member of the shelter community—even if she experiences some consequences of wife abuse that make her seem troublesome. When real women seemed to be not this type of person, when their behaviors could not be commonsensically understood as those of a battered woman, when their behaviors inspired anger rather than sympathy, then their membership in the battered woman social collectivity was lost. The interpretive device, in other words, could make sense of some unexpectable behaviors; it could not make sense of all such behaviors. Stated differently, when a woman's behaviors could be constructed as a consequence of wife abuse, then she remained a "battered woman" and she continued receiving sympathy even though she acted poorly. Conversely, when behaviors could not be so constructed—when the collective representation was threatened—she became described as a "not-battered woman." Rhetorically, therefore, shelter records confirm the characteristics of the battered woman type of person; in practice, women not meeting these expectations encountered worker anger and possibly eviction from the shelter.

For the battered woman type of person, the meaning of shelter work was confirmed. Workers did not need to concern themselves about women's complaints, troubles were neutralized, and continued sympathy and assistance were justified. But what about understanding the lack of success from this work? Neutralizing troubles is important but still, a social service provider who has trouble seeing many positive outcomes from her work is in a difficult position. So, I turn to the final issue: How workers could make sense of the fact that so few of their clients successfully transformed themselves into instances of the strong and independent woman.

Making sense of success

Former resident Margaret called—in a very hysterical state feeling overwhelmed with having no one to watch her sick child, not being able to go to work today, fearing the other kids would get sick, having no furniture, etc. etc. etc.

[467]

The collective representation of the battered woman type of person is of a woman needing only housing and support to achieve her goal of objective and subjective independence from abuse. Why, then, did not the housing and support offered by South Coast lead to considerable service success? Workers here constructed three ways to make sense of the disjuncture between expectations of success and the experience of lack of success.

First, although workers were oriented to the formal measure of success as *objective* independence from abuse, among themselves they most often defined success in terms of *subjective* independence. One worker told me:

I've had women that went back to their husband and I've felt good about it. There's something about when a woman is bordering on depression, she's had it, and you see her gradually come out of that and take control of her life and accept responsibility.

By such a definition, a client would be successful if she could be constructed as a woman who "had her head together." As another worker told me:

I think when you feel she's ready, whatever situation she's going to, even if she's going back to her husband or whatever, if she's got her head together enough so that she can cope with what she's got to face, we're successful.

Success by this definition would be unmeasureable, therefore, it would be achievable. As another worker said:

It gets into symbols, into mannerisms, what they're talking about, if there's been a break in their pattern of distress, if their faith has been restored.

While workers often implicitly juxtaposed the organizational measure of objective success with their measure of subjective success, their constructions were logical. Their measure was consistent with the organizational goal of producing strong women; it was consistent with worker activity oriented to changing women's subjective definitions of themselves. So, on a case by case basis, workers could construct their efforts as successful by constructing a client as a woman learning to define herself in organizationally approved ways:

Had a good talk with Helen. She talked about her feelings of resentment toward her husband and her low self-esteem. She is becoming increasingly aware.

[399]

They even could construct a successful client from a woman apparently far from being "happy":

She is very upset that her neighbor has turned on her and taken up with her boyfriend. She seems to want to begin anew and live more for herself—as in recognizing herself as an individual—that is very encouraging.

[417]

Second, but still within workers' constructions of success as subjective and unmeasureable, they could argue that success was a necessary outcome of shelter work. In so doing, they could argue *categorically* that South Coast "did a lot" for its clients:

Success is not going to be that nice family image with the white house and the picket fence and happy, smiling people. We've done a lot even if she does return.

They could argue that success was there even if it took a while, even if it was not visible:

We're in a position where you might not see results. However, five years from now this woman might remember something and it might have a real impact on her life, but you'll never know it.

So, success could be total:

I would say we're 100 percent successful in making at least a minute dent in how that woman looks at the world and who she is.

When workers defined success in subjective, unmeasureable terms, and when they defined it as a necessary outcome of shelter work, they could salvage the meaning of their work. But to be truthful, such talk was rare. Indeed, my examples of worker talk are from formal interviews where I explicitly asked them to define success. And, there were not many positive notes in the shelter log to give evidence for these constructions. Granted, there were notes happily reporting that one or another client had found an apartment or a job, that Legal Aid had accepted a particular case, that money had arrived from a relative, or that a woman was beginning to define herself a bit differently. Day-to-day there were small indications that worker efforts had yielded something. But this was not a final evaluation of "success." Indeed, workers had continuing evidence that their efforts were largely unsuccessful because most successful clients simply disappeared. Many such women moved out of the area to establish a new life elsewhere; even when women remained in the area, they rarely would contact this organization.[10] At the same time, unsuccessful clients tended to remain visible. Their names would appear in newspaper articles when police responded to new calls about wife abuse; they would call South Coast again and again requesting further help. The point is that, given the evidence, it was difficult to support *any* notion of success.

So, we come to a third orientation to success: Do not expect it, do not look for it, define it as non-pertaining to shelter work. As used by South Coast workers, this construction was supported both by the content of the battered woman collective representation and by the model of shelter work at South Coast.

First, denying the *possibility* of success was supported by the battered woman collective representation. After all, this type of woman is constructed as one beginning her life as an over-socialized girl; she is characterized by her *life-long* dependence and by what she lacks—self-esteem, skills for independent living, and modern consciousness about women's place. Although claims-makers, at least those who publicly advocate shelters, are prone to argue that such environmentally created characteristics can be changed simply by putting this woman into a new environment, workers at South Coast were practical actors who labeled this notion "naive":

> God, what can you do in thirty days? A person who took thirty or forty years to get where they are now, thirty days? You're not going

to change their entire life and send them out as whole persons with no problems.

Despite the good intentions of social problems claims-makers, the collective representation of the battered woman type of person leads to an image of such a woman as not a "whole person." It is logical to argue that thirty days is not sufficient to undo the damage created by a lifetime of negative experiences. So, although workers did not blame clients for this plight, the battered woman collective representation could be used to deny the possibility of success:

> It seems unrealistic given my knowledge about the cycles of violence and battered women and battering men and all that stuff, it would be unrealistic to think I'm going to cure these people in thirty days.

In this way, the characteristics of the battered woman type of person could neutralize workers' failures to transform such a woman into a strong and independent woman. After all, what else could be expected given that clients were so emotionally confused:

> I talked for a long time with Charlotte about the EXTREME danger she is in. I reiterated that we feel she should get out of town but I don't feel she is leaning in that direction. She still feels confused and not ready to make any permanent decisions.
>
> [522]

In the final analysis, this allowed workers to construct themselves as persons doomed to fail given the characteristics of their clients:

> Dee is real tearful and keeps talking about going back to husband, maybe today. The whole time I've talked with her, I knew all the persuading to come here and stay a few days wasn't going to make a bit of difference. I felt I was fighting a losing battle.
>
> [823]

Granted, workers here could talk about women's difficulties in finding housing and the means to material independence; they did justify some lack of success in terms of the larger social structure prohibiting women's independence. Yet it remains the battered woman collective representation, when used as an interpretive device to make sense of experience, allowed workers to account for the lack of success in terms of their *clients'* personal characteristics.[11]

Second, workers' denial of the *applicability* of success was supported by the philosophy underlying shelter work at South Coast. While it is clear these workers could be very directive with clients, while it is clear they regularly defied the formal organizational mandate promoting client self-determination, they nonetheless could reference this mandate when it came to accounting for the lack of success. Simply stated by one worker:

> You do what you can for them while they're here and you accept that they are responsible for their decisions to leave.

This was a comforting rhetoric when workers believed a client had made a bad decision:

> She went home to get her boy off to school and didn't come back. She said she knew if she saw him he would talk her into coming back. We had a long conversation trying to figure out if we should try to go get her or at least call and see if she was all right. But we decided it was her decision.

I have no data from the shelter log to support my point that workers were not oriented to success. But in many ways my lack of data *are* my data. In practice, most clients left South Coast without even a note in the log to mark their departure; workers rarely noted where clients were going, and if they did, they never included their opinions. Once a client left South Coast, workers' attention would turn to other clients and to whoever took the former client's place; the short time spent with most clients prevented clients from leaving a strong memory with workers; worker turnover prevented workers from developing an organizational memory of individual clients.

Summary

> First, street-level bureaucrats modify their objectives to match better their ability to perform. Second, they mentally discount their clientele so as to reduce the tension residing from their

inability to deal with citizens according to ideal service models.
Michael Lipsky, *Street-Level Bureaucracy*

It is not sociologically surprising that South Coast workers found it
was all too common for the organization to disappoint clients and for
clients to disappoint the organization. After all, this was an organization
for a particular type of woman while classic exemplars or textbook cases
of collective representations rarely exist in social life. My questions
about how workers repaired these disjunctures are both practically and
theoretically important.

Practically, it is obvious that in theory and in practice South Coast
was organized for a particular type of woman. All organizational goals,
rules, and workers' orientations centered on helping the "battered
woman"; the organizational design assumed clients would get along
together, keep the place clean and be engaged in the tasks of achieving
independence; obviously the organizational design assumed there would
be some measure of service success. Furthermore, although shelter work
involved long hours at minimum wage, it was assumed that the "pay"
for this work would come from elsewhere—client gratitude and the
knowledge that workers had helped women. Because the smooth operation of this place depended on clients who were more-or-less examples
of the type of person for whom the organization existed, questions about
disjunctures therefore are very practical. The more clients did *not* conform to this image, the more troubles there were—the more workers disappointed clients, the more clients disappointed workers, the more havoc
in the environment deemed so important to achieving service success,
the more workers could not construct their work as meaningful. Hence,
in practice, social service providers must reconcile disjunctures between
organizational guiding images and their practical experiences.

At South Coast, the organizationally approved way of making sense
of troubles was to use the collective representation of the battered
woman type of person as an interpretive device. This was a resource for
workers and it is not surprising that its use was associated with positive
outcomes for them *and* for clients. When workers made sense of trouble
and disappointment in this way, they constructed their work as meaningful; clients could continue receiving services although they defied the
norms of reciprocity in sympathy exchange. Yet the use of this device

was bounded. Not all clients' behaviors could be made sensible in terms of what is to be expected of a battered woman type of person. When the interpretive device could not commonsensically make sense of behavior then the client no longer was constructed as a "battered woman," no longer were sympathy and services mandated. This, too, was supremely sensible. As long as a woman was constructed as a battered woman, then workers had the mandate to offer her sympathy and support. But when this could no longer be done—when environmental havoc was intolerable, when other clients' safety was threatened, when anger was too high—workers *had* to construct her as "not-battered." This was the only way they could give themselves the mandate to withdraw sympathy and support because within South Coast it was morally unconscionable to deny services to a "battered woman."

A well-meaning reader might argue at this point that *all* victimized women should receive services regardless of their personal behaviors. While this is a powerful ideal, it would be difficult to achieve in the real world, especially in a place organized communally and with service ideals of self-help and peer support. Ideals and accompanying structure place limits on what types of behaviors can be allowed if the organization is to survive. Likewise, a well-meaning reader might argue that workers should never feel angry, that they should always feel sympathy toward their clients. This, too, is a powerful ideal but this, too, would be difficult to achieve in practice for two reasons. First, at least at South Coast, workers' emotional reactions toward clients were inextricably tied to their practical experiences. It was relatively rare for them to cast a woman as a "not-battered woman" merely because they did not "like" her. While there certainly are unexamined questions about how workers' general emotional reactions toward particular clients set in motion reflexive cycles of sympathy or antagonism, it remains that at least on-the-record and in worker talk there was a high association between negative emotions and client behaviors which, at least to workers, threatened South Coast in some way. Anger was experienced most often when a client was creating havoc for workers or for other clients, when she was not acting like a responsible member of the shelter community, when she refused to help herself, or when she acted as if South Coast was merely a cheap hotel. Worker anger, in other words, was tied to practical considerations—the very real needs to keep the place open, operating smoothly, and achieving the goal of helping the "battered woman." Second, to argue that workers should have always managed to feel sympathy is to imagine them as organizational robots. In practice, *real* social service providers are only more-or-less sensitive and forgiving, but they always are humans and as such they *will* experience emotional reactions toward their clients. Not all of these reactions will be organizationally approved.

What I am arguing here is a general point about modern-day social service organizations. All social services must begin operation with assumptions about their clients' characteristics, problems, and needs. Such assumptions *must* underlie organizational designs. Although social life always will be more complex, heterogeneous, and multidimensional than any image guiding a social service organization, guiding images become very real when they are institutionalized in the forms of organizational goals, procedures, and workers' orientations. Hence, social service organizations of all types will have disjunctures between images of client types and experiences and these disjunctures will create problems to be handled by social service workers who, as practical actors, are faced with the task of making sense of their clients and their work. This is the practical issue for shelters and for social services in general.

Theoretically, examining how workers reconciled disjunctures between expectations and experiences shows another aspect of how they rhetorically, and in fact, reproduced the collective image of the battered woman type of person. Simply stated, workers' accountings rhetorically reproduced the collective representation image of the battered woman as a good and grateful client. If she was troublesome, it was only because of the consequences of the condition known as "wife abuse." On-the-record, therefore, workers' experiences were reconciled with the collective representation. In the same way, women with characteristics and behaviors not seeable as those of a battered woman were constructed in purely behavioral terms. They were labeled as "angry and defiant," rule violations were noted, but such characteristics were *not* linked to the underlying condition of the "consequences of wife abuse." On-the-record, these women lost their membership in the battered woman social collectivity. Thus, the collectivity was protected, the "battered woman" was reproduced as a good and grateful client; disconfirming evidence either was incorporated within the category, or it was constructed as not pertaining. Such a rhetorical reproduction at South Coast was highly related to a reproduction of the social collectivity in fact: Women constructed as instances of the battered woman were forgiven for their transgressions; they continued receiving sympathy and support. Women losing their membership in this category faced a far different experience. They encountered angry workers and, in some instances, they were evicted—no longer were they shelter residents, no longer were they official members of the battered woman social collectivity.

Social service providers reproduce collective images when they repair disjunctures between expectations and experiences. This is the final and most sensible type of social problems work. In this instance, although South Coast endeavored to produce clients who were instances of the strong and independent woman, it was not for such a woman. Clients who criticized workers' interventions, rules or interpretations, clients presenting themselves as angry and defiant, clients who *were* constructed as strong and independent women lost worker support and organizational assistance. South Coast, in theory and in practice, was not a place for strong and independent women, it was not a place for all women needing housing, it was not a place for all victimized women. This was a shelter for the "battered woman."

From the perspective of those doing shelter work, this was how they made sense of their jobs. Day-by-day, these workers were engulfed in the tasks of shelter work, an unending work with a constantly changing, but never ending clientele. Workers could make their efforts meaningful only by faith in themselves and in their organization, only by the vague hope that some good was being accomplished, only by constructing their efforts toward individual women as charitable.

Chapter Seven

Social Problems Work and the
Reproduction of Public Problems

> . . . a sociology of social problems work grounded in
> Durkheimian sociology recasts claims-making activities as pro-
> cedures for producing and extending culture. In applying collec-
> tive representations and the social problems orientation to new
> aspects of everyday life, claims-makers simultaneously trans-
> form the objects, events, and persons being classified and give
> new practical meaning to the collective representations being
> applied.
>
> Gale Miller and James Holstein,
> "On the Sociology of Social Problems"

What *is* wife abuse? Who *is* the battered woman? These questions—and their answers—make visible aspects of late twentieth-cen-
tury American culture, and they demonstrate how the links between this
culture and social problems are forged, reproduced, and repaired.

Consider the implications of *asking* these questions. Simply asking
"what is wife abuse," or "who is the battered woman" implies these are
socially constructed categories; they are not Schutzian folk categories
arising naturally from practical experience.[1] Also implied by asking
these questions is what Mary Douglas calls a "complementary opposi-
tion": for there to be something called "wife abuse" and someone called
the "battered woman" there must be other conditions and people *not* of
these types.[2] Still further, since wife abuse and the battered woman are
social problem categories, they carry with them the evaluation of this
condition as morally intolerable, and the evaluation of this type of person as worthy of public assistance. Hence, asking these questions also

147

implies that not all conditions are morally intolerable and not all people are morally worthy. In brief, these commonly asked questions tell us that wife abuse and the battered woman are socially constructed categories of conditions and people set apart for special attention and moral evaluation.

Given that these categories are socially constructed, it is important to answer the recurring questions about their content. This was my first task and it was difficult because, like most social problems, no one person or group holds authority to make claims. Yet my general point, I believe, is supportable: As they have drifted into public consciousness, "wife abuse" and the "battered woman" are labels with *specific* contents. Not all violence is that of wife abuse, and not all victimized women are instances of the battered woman. My first questions were straightforward: What, specifically is being labeled as the morally intolerable violence called "wife abuse"; who, specifically, is being labeled as the "battered woman" who deserves public sympathy and assistance?

As constructed, wife abuse condemns as morally intolerable violence that is extreme, repeated, unstoppable and consequential; violence done by men on women for "no good reason." Thus, patriarchal schemes of interpretation defining men as "women's owners" are challenged. Also forcefully challenged are schemes of interpretation placing "family relationships" somewhere outside public concern and responsibility. And, since the logic of the collective representation leads to the prognosis that a woman must leave her partner, schemes of interpretation defining family stability as a primary value are challenged. At the same time, to say the condition called "wife abuse" is a social problem is not necessarily to condemn all violence; it is not to advocate public intervention into all family troubles. As constructed, the condition called "wife abuse" most clearly is about those incidents of violence that are most certainly outside popular notions of "normal violence." Explicitly and implicitly, wife abuse is about "not normal" violence.

It is easy to understand why this *particular* construction of wife abuse drifted into public consciousness. We only need to consider the possibility that alternative constructions would be viable. What are the chances, for example, that the American public could be convinced to condemn the types of violence now labeled as "normal," the types of violence occurring routinely in American homes? Unlikely. Or, what is the possibility that the public would give money to social services trying to help women leave their relationships because they had been "pushed" or "shoved" once or twice? This, too, is unlikely. Indeed, it was difficult enough for wife abuse claims-makers to convince the public that *extreme* violence should be condemned. Hence, while the shape of this public problem *was* constructed by social problems claims-makers, they could not construct any content they personally desired. Claim viability is decided by the American public; it reflects the larger culture.

The construction of the wife abuse problem is an example of the general tendency of social problems claims to construct extreme images of problematic conditions. For example, what is "child abuse?" Few Americans probably think of parental spanking in this category. No, in the popular imagination, "child abuse" is a label conjuring images of savage beating.[3] Or, who are "missing children?" I doubt the image coming immediately to mind is of teens who run away from their homes or of children taken by a non-custodial parent. No, the image is of children kidnapped by strangers, children then killed or sold into prostitution.[4] What is "poverty?" Here, the image is of people who are without homes, medical care or food; it is not an image of persons who live in too small houses, who have troubles finding medical care, and who eat cheap food. In each instance, the story is the same, and it is about Americans who tend to accept as social problems only those conditions that are well outside moral boundaries. Only at the extreme can enough worry be generated to support the social problem designation; only at the extreme do stories sell newspapers and magazines; only at the extreme do stories make good topics for talk shows and television movies. To be viable, social problems claims must convince enough social members that a condition at hand is intolerable and constructing the image of extreme conditions has the best chance of attaining this viability. Thus, just as *stranger rape* yields more public concern than does *date rape*, and just as *homelessness* is more compelling than *poverty*, which is more compelling than the problems of the *near poor*, as socially constructed, the public problem of *wife abuse* yields more concern than *normal violence* and this is more compelling than *marital troubles*.

Likewise, the specific content of the battered woman collective representation shows boundaries to Americans' willingness to offer sympathy. To say a battered woman deserves public sympathy and support is not necessarily to say that *all* victimized women have such a claim. As constructed, the battered woman deserves sympathy because she is in a dire situation, because she is a pure victim and because—for understandable reasons—she is unable to help herself. I am arguing here that what Candace Clark found to be the social rules surrounding the giving and getting of sympathy on an interpersonal level apply to *types* of persons.[5] The battered woman type of person was constructed as a woman in a dire situation, as not complicit in her plight and as morally pure. Hence, claims-makers did not change the social rules surrounding sympathy worthiness, they rather constructed the image of a "battered woman" to meet these implicit tests of sympathy worthiness.

Here, too, it is easy to see why this *particular* construction was publicly viable. Merely consider the possibility that many Americans would offer sympathy and services to a type of woman characterized as experiencing "normal violence," to a woman who was aggressive, domineering, or nagging. Probably not. Indeed, until the 1970s this *was* the image of victimized women. The public believed such a woman's victimization was not severe and that she "deserved" to be hit. No sympathy was forthcoming until the image of the victimized woman was changed, until the image of the "battered woman" was constructed.

This case, therefore, illustrates the importance of collective representations of people to the viability of social problems claims. Underlying all claims that a particular category of people deserves public sympathy are the implicit tests of sympathy worthiness. If the answer to any of these questions challenges claims to sympathy worthiness then sympathy can be withdrawn. So, for example, I would argue that persons living in near poverty are not the object of much public attention because, although their situation is unfortunate, it is not dire. It is clear that AIDS became a recognized social problem only when claims stressed its victims included heterosexuals, non-drug users, and children—categories of persons constructed as not complicit, categories removing the condition from the morally suspect categories of homosexuals and drug users. Likewise, homelessness became accepted as a social problem only when the image of such people as winos and bums was replaced with an image of them as guiltless women and children. Stated simply, social problems claims of any sort are the most viable when victims are constructed as the *type* of person who deserves sympathy.

I am arguing here that there are general themes in American culture leading to the situation that only particular kinds of images of conditions and people likely will foster public support for a social problem label. Certainly, there are claims and worry about conditions such as near poverty or violence against women. Such topics often are *sociological* problems, yet they tend not to be accepted as *social* problems in the public's imagination.

Hence, social problems are socially constructed. Out of the entire universe of conditions possibly pertaining, only a small portion come to public attention and become the object of public concern. Only a small portion of violence toward children is that of "child abuse," only a small portion of violence against women is that of "wife abuse," only a small portion of troublesome teenage behavior is that of "juvenile delinquency," and so on. Likewise, only some people who are poor are deemed worthy of sympathy, only some victimized women are instances of the "battered woman."

There are implications to this fact that social problems are constructed out of the heterogeneity and complexity of lived realities. At the level of social policy, for example, there is a tendency for policy to reflect the constructed images of problems rather than the underlying heterogeneity of lived realities. For the case at hand, the image of wife abuse as severe, frequent, consequential, and unstoppable violence has led to a focus on shelters for women who should and who must leave such a relationship; it has led to a focus on promoting police arrest and criminal prosecution of wife abusers. Likewise, the image of "missing children" as children in dire situations of danger has led to printing their pictures on milk cartons and on freeway toll tickets so that the public can look for them. In such instances, collective representations inform social policy and there are logical relationships between images of problems, persons, and policies to ameliorate problems. While, again, this is supremely sensible, it remains such policies will not be sensible for all potentially similar human troubles. Most certainly, social policy surrounding "homelessness" does nothing to assist a person who has a home that is all but uninhabitable. Or, we might ask whether or not public policy on the problem of missing children is correctly focused given that the great majority of such children are teenagers who choose to leave their homes, or children who are pawns in their parent's custody disputes. And, of course, we might ask about women experiencing violence. It makes sense that a woman experiencing the type of violence known as wife abuse would need a shelter; it makes sense to argue she should permanently leave her relationship; it makes sense that her abuser should be arrested and prosecuted since such violence obviously and clearly is criminal. But what about a woman who is "slapped" once or twice? Should *she* necessarily leave her relationship? Should police arrest, prosecute, and jail her abuser?

Thus, there is a logical and practical consequence of the American tendency to accept as social problems only extremely troublesome conditions and for policy to be informed by those particular conditions: Only persons experiencing these particular conditions become objects for public sympathy and support. And this has insidious implications. Does policy surrounding child abuse do anything for a child experiencing extreme "punishment?" Does policy on poverty or homelessness help persons who are "near poor?" Does policy on wife abuse help a woman experiencing "normal violence?" No. We wait until the child experiences *"child abuse"*; we wait until a person is *"homeless"*; we wait until a woman experiences *"wife abuse"*—and then we are concerned. This certainly is ironic. In the case of violence against women, if it is true as claims-makers argue that violence tends to increase in severity and frequency over time, if it is true that it becomes harder and harder to stop the violence the more it is patterned into the relationship, then we implicitly and explicitly tell victimized women to remain in their homes until they experience wife abuse. In the same way, we do relatively little to keep poor people *in* their homes. We wait until they are homeless.

A critical reader at this point likely will be thinking that this is the way it *should* be. The American ideal of individualism woven throughout our culture stresses that each person is responsible for her/himself and that it is not the public's responsibility nor even the public's right to intervene unless and until the condition becomes morally intolerable and persons become incapable of resolving their own problems. It is indeed true that this rhetoric of individualism is powerful; I am merely pointing out the implications.

Of course, a critical reader might now argue that, regardless of the power of the rhetoric of individualism, it nonetheless makes sense to focus resources and concern on those most in need. How would it make sense, for example, for a service provider to spend time with a child subjected to "severe punishment" when so many others are subjected to child abuse? How could a shelter worker in good conscience use scarce shelter resources to assist a woman experiencing "normal violence," when so many experience the brutalities of wife abuse? How could we justify worry about Americans living in inferior housing when so many are without housing? Under the condition of scarce resources for issues of social welfare such decisions are logical and sensible. Yet it remains: A victimized woman must buy her way into social services by showing us her bruises and broken bones; a person must experience the devastation of absolute poverty before assistance is provided; attention to prenatal nutrition and health care is by-passed in favor of resources to care for the tragic infants resulting from such ignored pregnancy. Regardless of the practical justifications we weave around our practices, it remains that Americans care little about prevention. We wait until heroic measures are needed although such measures are expensive and often doomed to failure since problems must be so extreme before they engage public attention and assistance. This, then, is a very practical implication of the social construction of public problems.

A second practical implication of the fact that public problems are socially and narrowly constructed pertains to the use of collective representations as interpretive devices to evaluate practical experience. While social problems claims-makers have the luxury—and the necessity—of bracketing heterogeneity in order to form clear and vivid images of the problem at hand, practical actors must undertake evaluations within lived realities where experiences do not come to us with labels attached explaining their meaning, and where people do not carry a scarlet letter indicating their membership category. True, labels for public problems such as "wife abuse," "child abuse," or "learning disabilities" are most-typically used *as if* such conditions are obvious, and *as if* such conditions are readily and easily recognizable in lived experience. But while there is a medical test for AIDS, and while we can be pretty sure when a teenager is pregnant, there is no x-ray, no test, no scientific formula for judging an individual person to be an alcoholic, a juvenile delinquent, or a battered woman; there is no line clearly differentiating odd behavior from mental illness, no line differentiating normal violence from child abuse or wife abuse. Hence, unique experience and unique persons must be evaluated and labeled and this is accomplished by matching lived realities with the collective representations.[6]

This is another reason why the specific content of collective representations is important. And here, again, implications arise from the tendencies of representations to be images of extreme conditions. For example, given the public image of *rape* as a *violent crime*, how likely is it that a woman who has been somewhat *forced* to engage in intercourse with her boyfriend will define herself or be defined by others as a "rape victim?" Is it likely a woman experiencing not-so-extreme, not-so-frequent and not-so-consequential violence will label herself or be labeled by others as a "battered woman?" Will a man who pushes around his wife define himself or be defined by others as a "wife abuser?" At the level of individual sensemaking, the extreme images of social problem conditions likely discourage practical actors from incorporating heterogeneous experience into these categories. Furthermore, collective representations painting images of persons in situations of most dire need, representations encouraging public support with images of people unable to help themselves also might prevent persons from incorporating *themselves* into these categories for another reason. The image of the battered woman is the case in point. Such an image does indeed encourage sympathy for such a woman but what woman would want to be known as such a person? As constructed, a battered woman is incompetent; she is unable to assist herself; she is out of touch with her own emotions. The image making such a woman into a person deserving sympathy simultaneously is an image of a less-than-adult person. The identity is discrediting, so it is no wonder that many women resist it.

In brief, for this analysis, I simply bracketed the very real problems of the objective condition known as "wife abuse." Yet there are practical implications of this examination of the social construction of public problems. Although social problems claims-makers in this instance have managed to convince many Americans that extreme, frequent, and consequential violence toward women does exist in all too many homes, although they have managed to convince many Americans that a woman experiencing such violence does need and deserve public assistance, this has not necessarily helped all victimized women. Women who have

been helped are those women whose experiences, biography, characteristics, and motivations do more or less conform to public images of wife
abuse and the battered woman. But what about women who do *not* conform to such images? What about women who are experiencing violence, but do not want or need a shelter? What happens to women who
are turned away from shelters such as South Coast because they are a
"not-battered woman?"

My interest here focused on the social *reproduction* of public problems within social service agencies. Most certainly, social problems
claims-makers do construct public problems. Out of the complexity,
multidimensionality and confusion of lived experience they define *a*
type of problem and *a* type of person. And, just as certainly, every time
a practical actor uses a social collectivity image to label a unique experience, the social collectivity is reproduced. But the story becomes more
complicated when the site for evaluation of practical experience is a
social service organization.

Formal social service agencies are critical sites for examining social
problems work. These places, simply stated, have powerful consequences for the people they do—and do not—serve. Most obviously,
only some women achieved entry to South Coast, others were turned
away. And, once a woman achieved entry to this place she was an official member of the battered woman social collectivity. As such, she
qualified for immediate food stamps, and her name went to the top of the
long waiting list for subsidized county housing. A woman turned away
did not enjoy this situation. Indeed, if the name of an official "battered
woman" went to the *top* of the waiting list for county housing, by definition, the name of a "not-battered" woman fell lower on the list. Furthermore, a woman achieving entry to this place also had worker support, and she went automatically into a referral network specifically for
the battered woman. The women turned away did not have this experience. In brief, just as to informally label a person as "poor" is much different from that person being so labeled by a government welfare
agency, to be officially labeled a "battered woman" was of practical sig-
nificance.

My story did not focus on the experiences of the women who used
South Coast services. Indeed, in order to examine shelter work from the
perspective of those doing this work, clients became shadowy characters

known only as they were constructed by workers. This examination was about workers' reality, it was not about the realities of women using these services. My primary concern was to trace through the reflexive relationships between social problems claims, the organization of social services, and worker practical activities and sense-making; my goal was to show how a type of public problem such as "wife abuse" and a type of person such as a "battered woman" are socially produced and reproduced. Regardless of whether or not workers reproduced the battered woman in fact—regardless of whether or not they actually did change clients' subjective and objective realities—they continually reproduced the wife abuse and battered woman collective representations rhetorically. I will end with an examination of this reflexivity in the production and reproduction of social problems. The links are many and complicated, and because reflexive examinations tend to yield convoluted writing, I have sketched an outline of my argument for readers to see at a glance these simultaneously reinforcing links between cultural interpretive schemes, collective representations, organizational design and worker activities and sense-making that together reproduce social facts. In this case, the social fact of the public problem of "wife abuse."

Reflexive analyses have no beginning. Indeed, that is the point: Social structure and social process together create and recreate social structure. But I will begin with the cultural background, the taken-for-granted interpretive schemes in the larger culture influencing the social problems work surrounding the public problem called "wife abuse."

First, the patriarchal scheme of interpretation and interpretations positively evaluating family privacy and stability were challenged by the wife abuse collective representation. But what was challenged was an *extreme* belief in male supremacy, and an *extreme* belief in the importance of family privacy and stability. That is, a social member can maintain some measure of belief in these traditional schemes, they can believe men *should* be in control, families *should* be private, and family stability *should* be valued, yet still suspend beliefs for the *extreme* condition of wife abuse. I would argue that the public's tendency to worry only about extreme conditions is reflected in the construction of "wife abuse," but so, too, is the lingering presence of beliefs in male supremacy and the importance of family privacy and stability. Stated otherwise, the wife abuse collective representation does not condemn all

Social Problems Work and the Reproduction of Public Problems

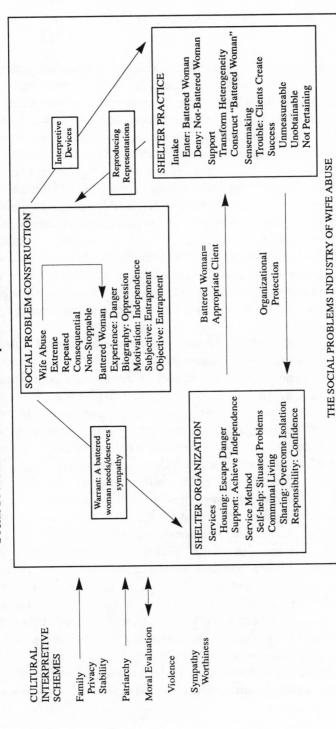

male dominance, it does not advocate public interference into all families, nor does it advocate marital breakup for all family troubles. If this is so, then these cultural interpretive schemes influenced the collective representation of wife abuse. At the same time, the social problems work surrounding wife abuse does *not* reproduce beliefs about the goodness of male control, family privacy, or family stability. On the contrary, the mere presence of shelters offers a continuing challenge to them. Every time a shelter offers a woman a chance to escape her victimization, every time workers advise a client that she should remain independent, every time workers manage to change bureaucratic social service rules to make women's independence a bit easier, the challenge is accomplished. So, while Americans' beliefs about gender and family no doubt encouraged wife abuse to be constructed as very extreme behavior, the social problems work surrounding this public problem does *not* reproduce those beliefs. On the contrary, this work offers a continuing challenge to them.

Two other interpretive schemes—the moral evaluation of violence and the moral evaluation of sympathy worthiness—are a *reflexive* part of the social problems work surrounding the wife abuse problem. First of all, the collective representations of wife abuse and the battered woman *reflect* these interpretive schemes. As constructed, wife abuse is about "not normal" violence, as constructed, the battered woman deserves sympathy. Likewise, other social problems work *reproduces* these interpretations. Rules and services at South Coast, for example, were justified as necessary for women experiencing "not normal" violence. Thus, the cultural interpretive scheme was embedded in the organizational design. Furthermore, on a case by case basis, workers at South Coast evaluated stories and people: Was *this* situation normal violence or not? Was *this* woman in a dire situation or not? Was *this* woman complicit in her plight or not? When a story and person could more-or-less be constructed as a story of "not normal" violence and a sympathy-worthy woman then the woman was labeled as a "battered woman" and she achieved South Coast entry. As long as workers continued to construct stories and women in these ways, membership in the battered woman social collectivity was maintained.

In brief, social problems work in this instance does not challenge cultural interpretations surrounding the moral evaluation of violence and people. Indeed, it confirms these interpretations. These interpretations are confirmed by the collective representations of wife abuse as "not normal" violence and the battered woman as "sympathy-worthy"; they are confirmed by shelters whose organization is specifically for such a woman with such an experience; they are confirmed by workers who distinguish between "wife abuse" and "not wife abuse," between a "battered woman" and a "not-battered woman." These cultural interpretive schemes *would* be challenged if wife abuse was clearly about "normal violence," if shelters were organized specifically for women experiencing such "normal violence," and if workers understood their job to be one of giving sympathy to women who were not in a dire situation and who were complicit in their plight. This is not the case. So, while it is certain that all too many women *do* meet these tests of the moral evaluation of violence and people, it remains that the social problems industry of wife abuse reflects *and* perpetuates the general cultural notions that some violence is acceptable and that only some people deserve sympathy.

My first comment is that social service agencies of any type are located within the larger culture. Images of problems, people, organizational design, worker activities, and sensemaking in various ways reflect *and* challenge or perpetuate larger cultural evaluations of problems and people.

Once inside the social problems industry there are many other reflexive and mutually supportive relationships among social problem collective representations, organizational form, and worker practical activity and sensemaking.

To set the stage, it is critical to remember that each social service is organized to assist a specific type of person. In modern day America there are no social services organized to help *any* person to do *any* thing. South Coast was organized specifically to help one type of person, "the battered woman," do one type of thing, "achieve independence." Organizational form, ideology, and method of service provision each were justified only for this type of person. So, workers believed the battered woman was different from the woman-in-transition, although both types of clients could reasonably be cast as "women in need of housing." In theory and in practice, South Coast was organized for the "battered woman."

Workers here never questioned the basic organization form. Granted, they continually tinkered with rules and procedures, but they never questioned the organizational ideals of self-help, communal living arrangements, and nonprofessional workers. And this is my point: What good would it have done for them to question these? These frontline workers were powerless to transform the organizational design. They could not, for example, transform South Coast into a luxury apartment building; clients *had* to live communally. Given so few workers and so much to do, they could not offer clients much individual attention; they *had* to rely on self-help and peer support. Although some clients complained that workers were not professionals, it is unlikely a professional person would work such long hours at minimum wage. South Coast workers were *not* professionals. Since there certainly was no budget to hire hotel maids, clients *had* to keep the place habitable. Now it is true that organizational ideals promoted self-help, peer support, nonprofessional workers, and communal living as good for the battered woman type of person but it remains that given organizational resources these *had to be*.

Also critical to my argument is that the organizational ideology, form, and method of service provision so sensible *given the collective representations* of wife abuse and the battered woman, supplied workers with rhetorical resources to make sense of the messiness of practical experience while this same ideology, form, and method of service provision constrained workers. Within any organizational framework—which, of course, always is located within the larger culture—service workers are practical actors. They are neither organizational robots nor free agents.

Within the organizational and cultural structure, South Coast workers actually accomplished shelter work for the battered woman. They officially admitted only some women to the shelter and hence to the official collectivity called the "battered woman," they continually constructed clients as instances either of a battered woman or a not-battered woman; they made sense of clients' personal characteristics, troubles, and the lack of service success in terms of this type of person. Although I focused on how workers used the battered woman collective representation as an interpretive device to justify and make sense of their experiences, decisions, and activities, this use, of course, disguised the fact that workers used folk knowledge to make such categorizations. On-the-record, a woman was constructed as a battered woman or a not-battered woman, but the grounds for such categorizations rested on folk knowledge workers called "vibes." Furthermore, workers' use of the collective representation disguised a political fact: a "battered woman" simultaneously was an "appropriate client." The use of this device allowed workers to deflect questions of how the *organizational* characteristics were compatible with some women's characteristics, problems, and needs, and incompatible with others'. When used as an accounting device, the battered woman collective representation furnished workers with a neat and tidy way to make sense of buzzing confusion and multiple relevancies. It allowed them to display to one another that their actions and decisions were in accord with the rule: This was a shelter for the battered woman. In the course of accomplishing this social problems work, workers reproduced the collective representations informing this place. In particular, they protected their organization by reproducing understandings that South Coast was properly organized and good for the battered woman and they reproduced the collective representations of wife abuse and the battered woman.

Workers protected their organization in three ways. First, in their actions and justifications, they reproduced the belief that South Coast offered the battered woman what she wanted and needed. If a particular woman did not seem to want or need what the organization offered, then workers constructed her either as "emotionally confused"—a characteristic of the battered woman making it possible to deny the validity of her perspective—or they constructed the woman as not-battered—a type of woman for whom the organization was not designed. Although I certainly do *not* claim these workers actually accomplished their goal, it is certain they tried to allow entry to women who seemed to want and need what South Coast offered and they tried to deny entry to women who seemed to want or need something else. Regardless of the extent to which they accomplished this in fact, it remains the organization was protected rhetorically. Rarely questioned by workers was the possibility that a victimized woman might *reasonably* and *justifiably* want something other than what this organization offered; rarely questioned was that a "not-battered" woman might *reasonably* and *justifiably* have a claim to organizational resources. Thus, workers protected the organization in fact when they denied entry to women constructed as not wanting or needing what South Coast offered; they protected the organization rhetorically when they constructed the appropriate client as a "battered woman"—a woman wanting and needing precisely what South Coast offered.

Second, workers reproduced the image of this organization as properly organized when they constructed interpersonal trouble either as due to an offending client's situation—understandable for a battered woman—or as due to her status as a "not-battered" woman. A troublesome client who was "not-battered" could justifiably be denied admission or evicted and hence, all troubles were made understandable in terms of the client. Again, while I do *not* claim that workers managed to neatly deflect all trouble this way, it remains they could, and did, deny entry or banish women challenging the ideal that South Coast was properly organized. Not entertained much by workers was the possibility there was something about the organization or about workers' behaviors that created troublesome clients; not entertained was the possibility that a "battered woman" might have morally contaminating personal characteristics *independent* of her victimization. Regardless, trouble was neutralized and South Coast remained constructed as properly organized for the battered woman.

Third, workers also reproduced belief in their organization by their accounting for organizational success—or the lack of it to be precise. Here they maintained success could be measured in non-measurable terms of subjective change, so important for the battered woman; conversely, they claimed success was impossible due to the characteristics of the battered woman, or they claimed success was not pertaining given the organizational mandate to allow clients the right to self-determination. Each of these accountings, of course, protected workers from considering another possibility: Perhaps they should be doing something other than what they were paid to do; perhaps success was more possible within a different kind of organization.

Each of these examples are variations on the same theme: In myriad ways, workers accomplished the social problems work of protecting the organization from evidence challenging the correctness of organizational ideology and form. Hence, they reproduced the belief that shelters are organized and effective for the battered woman. Critically, this was accomplished *not* primarily by modifying collective representations to fit practical experience; it was accomplished primarily by bringing experience into line with collective representations. While Alfred Schutz has argued that collective representations will be modified by practical experience this is not so possible in social service agencies where organizational *structure* determines what is and is not possible or likely. It is easier within such organizations to bring experience into line with structure than to bring structure into line with experience.

These frontline workers also reproduced the content of the collective representations of wife abuse and the battered woman. They did this when they accounted for their practical decisions and when they rhetorically transformed the heterogeneity of individual clients into the homogeneity of a type of person and a type of problem.

I will begin again with organizational structure. Consider, for example, the complex task of bringing in new clients. Clearly, this hated task was necessary given that South Coast had only so much room, given that only some services were available and given that clients had to have the personal skills to live communally. True, more clients could have been served if the organization had been larger, but, even if this place had been infinitely expandable, the notion of appropriate client would remain. Regardless of space, an appropriate client would continue to be a woman who wanted and needed what the organization had to offer; she would be a woman who could live among other women, she would be a "battered woman." My point is that the organizational structure determined what types of women could—and could not—be served.

Given this, workers went out into the world and attempted to select women who could be served. And, in their accounting for their decisions, workers constructed themselves as responsible representatives of a shelter for the battered woman. Allowed to enter, on-the-record, were women in situations of extreme danger, women who seemed pure victims of repeated assault, and women who wanted and needed this organization for the purpose of achieving independence—the "battered woman." Indeed, the more a petitioner was constructed as conforming to this image, the higher her priority, to the point that a woman constructed as a classic exemplar of a battered woman would achieve entry despite extreme overcrowding. Conversely, a petitioner constructed as a woman not experiencing repeated and brutal victimization, a woman constructed as strong and capable, or a woman constructed as not wanting help to achieve independence could justifiably be denied entry *regardless* of space availability.

Of course, such accounts by workers for their decisions are sensible. By their accountings, they offered shelter to women most in need of what the organization had to offer. Yet just as certainly, this was accomplished by transforming the heterogeneity of petitioners' complex stories into the homogeneity of a "battered woman" or a "not-battered woman." The complex process of sifting through biographies with often conflicting indicators was disguised and all that remains on-the-record is that a battered woman was allowed entry, a not-battered woman was deflected. Also as certain, in their justifications, workers reproduced the wife abuse and the battered woman collective representations. Simply stated, "wife abuse" *will remain* characterized as extreme, repeated victimization on women who are pure victims as long as women with other imputed characteristics are denied entry to the collectivity with the label "not-battered." And, just as clearly, the "battered woman" *will remain* characterized as a woman who desires independence but who is too weak to achieve it on her own as long as women describable in other terms are denied entry to the collectivity with the label "not-battered." This is the reproduction of the collective representations of wife abuse and the battered woman.

Workers also reproduced collective representations of the subjectivities of the "battered woman" when they constructed their clients in terms of emotional upsets, tearfulness, and confusions. Likewise, the collective representation was reproduced when women evaluated as angry, strong, or defiant were described in terms other than those of a battered woman. So, when individual clients were constructed as emotionally confused, such clients were incorporated into the "battered woman" social collectivity *and* this collective representation was reproduced. Clients constructed as strong, angry, and defiant tended to be excluded from this collectivity which kept such women and such emotions outside the collective representation of the "battered woman." So, the battered woman *will remain* characterized as a passive, confused, and somewhat hopeless creature as long as other constellations of subjectivities serve to deny their holders entry into the collectivity. This, too, is the reproduction of the collective representation of the battered woman.

This is the social problems work of frontline workers who, in the course of making sense of the buzzing confusion of experience effectively reproduce collective representations and hence, effectively reproduce public images of social problems. This work clearly is reflexive. How do we know the characteristics of wife abuse and the battered woman? We know by the claims made about such a condition and such a person. What is the evidence for these claims? Primarily the stories of *women residing in shelters*. The experiences and characteristics of women residing in such places—supported, of course, by the understandings of social service providers assisting these women—become the evidence supporting the social construction of wife abuse as severe, repeated, unstoppable behavior; they are the evidence supporting the construction of the battered woman as a pure victim who is unable to act on her own behalf; they are the evidence justifying the correctness of shelter organizations. In turn, the work in such places reproduces the cultural belief that only some violence is morally intolerable and that only some victimized women deserve public sympathy.

Despite the complexities in a reflexive analysis, it is all perfectly logical. There is a specific type of person and for this person there is a specific type of social service and within this social service workers do what they have to do. Social structure and social process hence reproduce images of types of people and types of problems. It is the social problems industry—claims-makers, organizational designers and frontline workers—who together produce and reproduce collective representations. Out of the buzzing confusion, heterogeneity, and complexity of lived realities a type of experience and a type of person is produced and reproduced. In the final analysis, it is social problems work that answers the questions of my students: What *is* wife abuse? Who *is* the battered woman?

Appendix

Data and Data Collection at South Coast

Chapters 3 through 6 use data from one shelter I call "South Coast." These data were collected over a period of about two-and-a-half years. During the first year, funding for an evaluation of the South Coast umbrella organization was provided by the Law Enforcement Assistance Administration (Richard A. Berk and Sarah Fenstermaker, Principle Investigators). After that, I volunteered for several months and continued working at this shelter. Then, the organization employed me for several more months as an internal evaluator and organizational record keeper. Then, I maintained my involvement as a volunteer for about a year after that. The moral of my story is clear: I cannot easily answer questions about my role at this place.

For my examination of this shelter I will, of course, protect client and worker confidentiality throughout. I will not specify when these data were collected and I will change the names of all clients as well as anything unique about them that could lead to their identification.

I will be using several forms of data to examine this organization. First, early on I did formal interviews with frontline workers, shelter supervisors, and the umbrella organization administrators. This was during the time when South Coast was first taken over by the umbrella, and with all the ensuing publicity, the shelter was experiencing an ever-increasing demand for its services. Workers and administrators came to the conclusion that perhaps the time had come for some formal guidelines or limits on the number of clients who could be served, since everything had been very undefined prior to that time. So, I interviewed workers in order to understand their perspectives about what and how limits could be placed on services. In these interviews I asked each worker one primary question: "If two women called and requested shelter and for some reason you could admit only one of them, how would you decide which woman to admit?" With each response I asked again,

"Well, suppose these two women were the same on that—then what might you look for?" Commonly, workers resisted the notion that some women could be turned away, yet each did construct lists of priorities. Along the way, they also talked about how they made decisions and their philosophies of shelter work ran throughout their comments. My main finding was that workers believed only they could make these judgments and that judgments were totally situated. Workers' arguments were so convincing that administrators decided to leave all such decision-making in the hands of workers.

Second, although my primary concern is in how the battered woman type of person has been constituted as an *object* of social problems work, from time to time I will allude to demographic characteristics of women who used South Coast services. This information is from Client Information Forms completed when women entered and when they left this shelter.

I have two primary forms of data for this analysis. The first are notes from the shelter *logbook*, a worker-written ongoing commentary about life inside South Coast. This organizational document was compiled by workers and only workers could read its contents. The log served the practical purpose of allowing communication among revolving shifts of workers, who rarely saw one another but who were engaged in the common task of shelter work. As an organizational document, the log was merely a loose-leaf binder of blank pages to be filled by workers in free-form writing. An entry could be a few words or a whole page, notes could contain profanity or poetry, commonsense or clinical reasoning. The log was compiled by workers for an audience of other workers, so entries were written and evaluated by an audience of insiders to shelter work. There was only one rule about what should be written: Workers were to keep one another informed about anything that might affect others on upcoming shifts. Entries could describe interpersonal problems inside the shelter, efforts of workers to assist clients, activities of clients, instructions to workers on upcoming shifts, mundane problems with plumbing or mice, notes about callers who requested but who were denied shelter, interactions with former or potential clients, and notes about new clients allowed entry.

After I had worked at South Coast for some months, workers loaned me several of these binders saying that the logbook was the best information available about this place. To them, the log showed what shelter work was *really* like. I immediately took these to my office and typed verbatim all the worker scrawled notes (the behavior of a graduate student), so what I have are 540 pages of single-spaced copy separated into days. I consecutively numbered these days beginning with 324 (a number having an empirical referent only in my research) and ending with day 840, which just happened to be the last day in one of the binders. Throughout this work I will include a notation of the day in which the cited log entry appeared. I do this to allow readers to see that although South Coast experienced three complete turnovers of workers and supervisors during this time the general themes remained.

What do these log entries represent? Certainly, they do *not* offer an "objective" or a "researcher" view of this organization. Workers would write what they personally believed other workers needed to know but this "need to know" was situated and depended on such things as how busy workers were—there were more entries on slow days than on hectic ones. Predictably, problematic and unexpected occurrences found their way into this document more than did non-problematic and routine happenings.

To an outsider, the log is frustrating. There are irritating patterns of missing information, often a day's work or an hour's conversation is summarized in a few words or lines. The log, in brief, is not the same as a good set of field notes. But that is why it is a fascinating source of data. It is the story of shelter work from the perspective of those who do this work.

Last, but certainly not least, my field notes are the second major form of data I will be using. These notes sometimes are from staff meetings where workers allowed me to tape their deliberations, some are from interactions with workers or clients I managed to transcribe verbatim since I take shorthand. Yet most of my several hundred pages of field notes are not so detailed. I decided quite early that many of the most critical happenings at South Coast could not be turned into data collection events. For example, although I witnessed several client selection decisions and, in fact, was responsible for a few myself, I neither took notes nor turned on my tape recorder during these times. Nor did I take notes while listening to workers and clients talk. I always went home or to my office and reconstructed what I had seen or experienced.

Of course, I would be thrilled to have actual transcripts of critical events but I still believe it was not possible to gather more exact data for two reasons. First, I made an implicit bargain with workers who were not prone to trust researchers and who had no love of graduate students either. My deal with them was that if I acted like a shelter worker they would let me hang around, and they would trust me. To turn on a tape recorder or to take notes when a worker would be handling the situation would have been to wear out my welcome. So, there were the usual issues of maintaining access, complicated in an organization where workers were obsessed with not turning the organization or its clients into research subjects.

That said, I will admit that even if there had not been a problem of maintaining access, even if workers had been amenable to research, I could not have transformed much of what I saw, heard, and experienced into "scientific data." What I personally experienced during my involvement with South Coast clearly affected my data and what I experienced was a severe disjuncture, the schizophrenic experience of living in two different worlds. One was the world of South Coast, a world of chaos and crisis, noise and dirt, of immediate practical action in confusing situations. My other world was a quiet and clean university office with its file cabinets, books, and computer, a world of reflection. My intellectual project required *data*, but data were relevant only when I was at my office. While at South Coast, I witnessed an ongoing, emotionally riviting soap opera. True, I did begin my association with this place primarily as a student interested in work so I could pay my rent, but it was only a matter of weeks before the organization, its people, and its clients were no longer abstractions or means to an end. Before long, I began to question the value of academic analysis in a world of immediacy, crisis, want, and pain. Thus, my field notes come and go in their clarity. Sometimes I retreated to my office and when I reemerged I took good notes for a while. At other times, I got swept up in the problems of the moment and data collection seemed simply irrelevant.

In summary, depending on my mood, I evaluate my data either as terrible or very good. They are terrible when I judge them using traditional criteria. For example, since much of my data come from workers, it is disturbing that they were, shall we say, very poor record keepers; my field notes contain all sorts of fascinating stories yet rarely can I offer a moment-by-moment description of how a particular event unfolded; my notes range from those that could demonstrate how field notes should look to those merely demonstrating the problems of going native. When viewed from the outside by traditional methodological criteria, my data are not good and I can say only that what I lack in quality data I make up by the fact that I collected a great quantity and diversity of data from this place.

At the same time, it remains that for my particular project my data are very good, since they represent shelter work from the perspective of those actually doing this work rather than from the perspective of those merely studying it. So, if workers typically did not collect some forms of information, it is because it did not matter to them; if log entries do not reveal the order of interaction, it is because only the final outcome mattered; if entries are too cryptic for outsiders, it is because outsiders do not share workers' understandings. My data from South Coast make perfect sense to frontline service providers doing this work. If they are incomplete from the perspective of outsiders, it is because outsiders are engaged in a different enterprise. It is the enterprise of *doing* shelter work that I attempt to examine.

NOTES

Introduction

1. Ian Hacking, "Making Up People," p. 222-236.

2. See Elizabeth Pleck, *Domestic Tyranny*, for a complete history of this problem throughout American history. See Susan Schechter, *Women and Male Violence*; Marlena Studer, "Wife Beating as a Social Problem"; and Kathleen Tierney, "The Battered Women Movement," for more detailed examinations of the specific claims-making activities leading to public consciousness that "wife abuse" was a social problem rather than an individual trouble.

3. Gale Miller and James A. Holstein, "On the Sociology of Social Problems," p. 4.

4. I am using the terms "collective representations" and "interpretive structures" as they are used by Gale Miller and James A. Holstein in "On the Sociology of Social Problems." Their framework is Durkheimian because collective representations are understood to reflect social structure, in that they embody shared understandings; their framework simultaneously is compatible with Alfred Schutz's phenomenological interest in how social members use interpretive structures to make sense of practical experience.

5. Harold Garfinkel, *Studies in Ethnomethodology*, p. 76-103.

6. Kathleen Ferraro, "Processing Battered Women," p. 423.

7. According to Joseph Gusfield, "On the Side," p. 46-48, the social construction approach, although often criticized for its apparent lack of a moral message, *is* critical of the social problems industry itself. According to him:

> In scrutinizing the definition of problems and claims of problem professionals, the sociologist becomes the critic of the effort of public agencies and associations to make legitimate claims to solve social problems as technical problems, as the domain of the professional.

Wife abuse has become a social problems industry in that careers can be built from it. Some persons now specialize in counseling the "battered woman," others have built careers representing such women in court, others have built careers writing about this topic, and still others of us have built careers researching it.

Chapter 1

1. It would be hopeless and nonproductive to filter claims through a precise definition of feminism, since there is little agreement on what, precisely, feminist claims about "wife abuse" and the "battered woman" look like. I will illustrate this point with one example: In their review of the literature, Wini Breines and Linda Gordon, "The New Scholarship on Family Violence," claim that Lenore Walker's, *The Battered Woman*, concept of "learned helplessness" is an example of feminist claims. Yet Laurie Wardell and her colleagues in "Science and Violence Against Wives," conversely define this same concept as sexist and not feminist because it can be interpreted as a characteristic of a battered woman that encourages her victimization and thus it deflects blame from the abuser to the victim. See Michelle Fine, "Unearthing Contradictions"; and Susan Schechter, *Women and Male Violence*, for examinations of competing feminist visions of the problem called "wife abuse." Also, there are continuing debates about the consequences of such diversity. Kathleen Tierney, "The Battered Woman Movement," for example, argues that diversity among wife abuse claims-makers has led to broad-based support for this problem. Yet Patricia A. Morgan, "Constructing Images of Deviance"; and John M. Johnson, "Program Enterprise," believe such diversity has been detrimental, for it has led to a rapid dilution of the original radical feminist claims about this social problem.

2. I want to show how similar images appear in different types of magazines. Therefore, I will cite article titles and magazine names in my notes. The reference list likewise will be arranged by magazine title, and I shall note any bylines there.

3. In the following chapters, I will be illustrating how claims can be translated into social service organizational form. Since my exemplar shelter, South Coast, was organized in the late 1970s, it seemingly would be sensible to use only claims appearing before that time. But I want to at least implicitly show how little claims have changed over time. So, I will include in my references more current claims. Furthermore, the redundancy of claims is overpowering

and my interest is not in examining claims made by any one specific claims-maker. Therefore, I will not cite every claims-maker on every point. Readers who are interested in examining more-or-less complete sets of claims about wife abuse and the battered woman should see R. Emerson and Russell P. Dobash, *Violence Against Wives*, for a tightly argued feminist academic work; Del Martin, *Battered Wives* , for what often is called the "classic activist" statement; Jennifer Baker Fleming, *Stopping Wife Abuse*, for a service provision slant; Mildred Daly Pagelow, *Family Violence*, for a college textbook rendition; Lenore Walker, *The Battered Woman*, for what is probably the most often quoted work, and Elizabeth Pleck, *Domestic Tyranny*, for a complete treatment of the history of this problem and public response to it.

4. The label for the social problem category called "wife abuse" denotes the potential relevance of both gender and family. Therefore, it raises a question about which category system is *most* relevant to the problem at hand. Only a few claims-makers define "wife abuse" as a type of *family* abuse (e.g. Murray A. Straus, et. al., *Behind Closed Doors*); a few others relabel the problem as "woman abuse" to emphasize *gender* (e.g. Mildred Daly Pagelow, *Woman-Battering*; Susan Schechter, *Women and Male Violence*). Most claims-makers circumvent this question of what is the *most* relevant by collapsing family into gender. This is accomplished by explicitly redefining "wife" to include women in *any* type of cross-sex relationship (e.g. Donna M. Moore, "An Overview"; Lenore Walker, *The Battered Woman*).

5. For example, at the U.S. Civil Rights Commission hearings, one woman began her testimony by saying she already had a master's degree when she "got into this situation (Faith Spotted Eagle, "Testimony," p. 115-117); at the U.S. House of Representatives hearing, *Dr.* Toby Myers offered her personal testimony (Toby Myers, "Testimony," p. 184). See also: "Battered Wives" *U.S. News*; "Powerless in the Suburbs" *McCalls*; and Lenore Walker's, *The Battered Woman*, chapter on "Myths and Reality" for examples of how emphasis is placed on incorporating affluent women into the category of battered woman.

6. This is a critical claim and one meeting empirical challenge when Murray A. Straus and his colleagues in *Behind Close Doors*, made public data seemingly showing that inside homes women were as violent as men and hence, there were as many "battered husbands" as "battered wives." The wife abuse claims-makers question such data in terms of its methodological and conceptual validity (see Wini Breines and Linda Gordon, "The New Scholarship on Family

Violence"; Elizabeth Pleck et. al., "The Battered Data Syndrome"). In general, these claims-makers argue that women are *not* violent and/or that women's violence is limited to self-defense, and/or that women's violence is not consequential (e.g. Carol Nadelson and Maria Sauzier, "Intervention Programs"; Susan Schechter, *Women and Male Violence*. Also, see Daniel G. Saunders, "Wife Abuse, Husband Abuse," for a recent review of feminist criticisms of the "mutual combat" construction and see Mildred Daly Pagelow, *Family Violence*, p. 273-277, for a critical examination of the "battered husband" collective representation.)

7. All wife abuse claims share this understanding that women are the pure victims. See Wini Breines and Linda Gordon, "The New Scholarship on Family Violence," p. 518; Dorie Klein, "Can This Marriage"; R. Emerson and Russell P. Dobash, *Violence Against Wives*; Laurie Wardell et. al., "Science and Violence"; Susan Schechter, *Women and Male Violence*; and Michele Bograd, "Family Systems," for the feminist logic underlying this "woman as victim" stance.

8. For illustrations of professional and affluent men who are wife abusers see "At Last We Have Hope," *McCalls*, p. 25; "Wife Abuse," *Christianity Today*, p. 23; "A Troubled Double Life," *Time*; and "A Private Crisis," *Newsweek*.

9. Lenore Walker, *The Battered Woman*, p. xv. For explicit claims that wife abuse is a label for acts where a man intends to do violence for the purpose of control, see Mildred Daly Pagelow, *Family Violence*, p. 327; "Why Men Hurt," *Readers Digest*, p. 78; "How to Recognize," *Glamour*, p. 209; "At Last We Have Hope," *McCalls*, p. 26. I should mention that most claims-makers do not deny commonsense associations between the acts called "wife abuse" and "alcohol" or "stress." Many illustrations do involve drunkards and/or men who can be seen as suffering from stress. What claims-makers *do* object to is the idea these somehow excuse the behaviors called "wife abuse."

10. Most often, this is associated with academic feminist claims labeling *anything* serving to control women as woman abuse. Within these constructions, male violence is called a "unitary phenomenon," and all women living in patriarchal societies are therefore abused. The term "abuse" in this particular framework is used to label phenomenon such as "rape," "pornography," the "structure of employment," "psychosurgery," "sexual harassment," "medical control of reproduction" and so forth. See, for example, the volume edited by

Jalna Hanmer and Mary Maynard, *Women, Violence and Social Control.*

11. For example, Michele Bograd, "Feminist Perspectives," p. 12, defines wife abuse as the "use of physical force"; Dorie Klein, "Can This Marriage," defines it as a "physical assault"; John Flynn, "Recent Findings," defines it as a "physical attack." James H. Scheuer, Chair of the U.S. House of Representatives Committee on Domestic Violence, "Comments," p. 146, offered his "layman's definition" of wife abuse.

12. Nanci Clinch, "Testimony"; and Marta Segovia-Ashley, "Testimony," p. 100.

13. "Why Men Hurt," *Readers Digest*, p. 79.

14. Del Martin, *Battered Wives*; Lenore Walker, *The Battered Woman*; Mildred Daly Pagelow, *Woman-Battering*. See also Dorie Klein, "Can This Marriage"; and Roger Langley and Richard C. Levy, *Wife Beating*, who follow the convention of beginning their claims about wife abuse with personal stories.

15. Del Martin, *Battered Wives*, p. 1-2. It is of interest to note that opening with personal stories is a quite common claims-making technique for all types of social problem constructions. According to Joel Best, "Rhetoric in Claims-Making," such a technique subtly encourages readers to view the personal story as "typical."

16. For such explicit claims see Steven M. Morgan, *Conjugal Terrorism*, p. 2.

17. "Why Men Hurt," *Readers Digest*, p. 78; personal testimony of Toby Myers, "Testimony," p. 184-185.

18. Lenore Walker, "Testimony," p. 146.

19. Many claims on all stages of social problem construction contain such examples. I have used claims from the following articles and magazines: "Northern Ireland," *Ms.*, p. 98; "London," *Ms.*, p. 24; "Scarred Lives," *Glamour*, p. 56. For other examples see Lenore Walker's, *The Battered Woman*, chapters on "Sexual Abuse" and "Economic Deprivation."

20. Although it is true that I've chosen vivid illustrations, I did not misrepresent the force of these claims. For example, see chapter 5 in Lewis Okun's, *Woman Abuse*, for a graphic listing of what he terms the "chillingly creative, sophisticated, morbid and sadistic torture techniques" used against the battered woman.

21. R. Emerson and Russell P. Dobash, *Violence Against Wives*, p. 1; Marjory Fields, "Testimony," p. 20; "Battered Women," *Essence*, p. 75.

22. All claims focus on repeated violence, many explicitly define "wife abuse" as repeated victimization and/or explicitly reserve the label of "battered woman" for women who have experienced such repeated victimization. See Kathleen J. Ferraro and John M. Johnson, "How Women Experience Battering"; Erin Pizzey, "Pizzey Comments"; Lenore Walker, *The Battered Woman*.

23. Lewis Okun, *Woman Abuse*, p. 77 claims: "There is a great consensus in the woman abuse literature . . . that conjugal violence tends to increase in both its severity and frequency as the battering relationship continues over time." See also R. Emerson and Russell P. Dobash, *Violence Against Wives*, p. 124; "Curbing the Wife-Beaters," *MacLeans*.

24. Because he typically denies there are any problems with his behavior and/or believes his behavior is not his fault, claims-makers argue that an abusive man is a very poor research subject. See Mildred Daly Pagelow, *Family Violence*, p. 336; and James Ptacek, "Why Do Men Batter Their Wives?" for reviews of such claims. The poor prognosis for change runs throughout. Mildred Daly Pagelow, *Family Violence*, p. 336, argues "nine out of ten such men will not change." It also seems Lenore Walker's "cycle of violence" theory, *The Battered Woman*, has reached a taken-for-granted status among claims-makers. Walker argues that wife abuse is characterized by three phases: tension-building, violence, and loving respite where the abuser feels guilty and promises to reform. R. Emerson and Russell P. Dobash, *Violence Against Wives*, also claim their research shows periods of relative calm in marriages containing wife abuse. Yet all claims-makers argue violence *will* eventually resume. Simply stated in "How to Recognize," *Glamour*, p. 207: "The beating-remorse-beating cycle is endlessly repeated." Therefore, according to Betsy Warrior, *Working on Wife Abuse*, p. 75; and "If You Loved Me," *Redbook*, p. 105, a woman's hopes that her partner will change are a "false and futile dream."

25. Donna M. Moore, "An Overview," p. 8; Steven Morgan, *Conjugal Terrorism*, p. 2. Both these works argue the "presence of physical damage is important because it satisfies the definition used by police and courts"; Elaine Hilberman, "Sixty Battered Women," p. 1338 claims "serious and/or repeated injury" is the generally accepted definition among those who treat victims of wife abuse. One claims-maker, however, argued in a policy hearing that injuries might be "not currently physically apparent" since abusers often hit women in

the abdomen and other areas hidden by clothing (Yolanda Bako, "Testimony," p. 67).

26. Del Martin, *Battered Wives*, p. 1.

27. "Battered Wives," *U.S. News*, p. 47; "I Was a Battered Wife," *Good Housekeeping*, p. 34.

28. See, for example, "On Being An Abused Wife," *Mademoiselle*; "Life in a Domestic Hell," *MacLeans*; "If You Loved Me," *Redbook*; and "I Don't Want," *Ladies Home Journal*. The traditional notion that a battered woman somehow *likes* to be abused now is called the "myth of masochism." On all stages of social problem construction, claims-makers are careful to challenge this idea. Their specific illustrations involve women who most assuredly do *not* like their abuse and among academic claims-makers there are articles devoted specifically to constructing what might appear to be masochism as an indication of an underlying "enforced restriction of choice." See Elaine Hilberman, "Overview"; and Elizabeth Waites, "Female Masochism," for more complete claims about what is called the "myth of masochism."

29. For further discussion of what are now called the "myths of wife abuse" see Lenore Walker, *The Battered Woman*, chapter 1; and Richard J. Gelles and Claire Pedrick Cornell, *Intimate Violence*, p. 13-20.

30. This claim about what a battered woman should do runs throughout. See Marjory Fields, "Testimony," p. 26; and Marta Segovia-Ashley, "Testimony," p. 103, for claims made in public policy hearings; Elizabeth Waites, "Female Masochism"; and Bruce J. Rounsaville, "Theories of Marital Violence," for examples of claims written by and for academics; Susan F. Turner and Constance Shapiro, "Battered Women," p. 372; and Jerry Finn, "The Stresses and Coping Behavior," for social work claims; "On Being An Abused Wife," *Mademoiselle*; and "If You Loved Me," *Redbook*, for magazine examples.

31. Most claims-makers attend to this issue of why women stay. This attention becomes a specific topic for academic journal articles (e.g. Mildred Daly Pagelow, "Factors Affecting"; Michael J. Strube, "The Decision to Leave"; Michael J. Strube and Linda S. Barbor, "Factors Related"; Del Martin, "What Keeps a Woman Captive"; Richard J. Gelles, "Abused Wives"; Kathleen J. Ferraro and John M. Johnson, "How Women Experience"); also chapters in books (e.g. Mildred Daly Pagelow, *Woman-Battering*; Lewis Okun, *Woman*

Abuse; Terry Davidson, *Conjugal Crime*; Del Martin, *Battered Wives*; Roger Langley and Richard C. Levy, *Wife Beating*); and magazine articles (e.g. "Why Women Stay," *Essence*; "I was a Battered Wife," *Ladies Home Journal*; "He Beat Me," *Vogue*; "Battered Wives," *Psychology Today*; "Battered Women," *Ebony*).

32. "New Hope for the Battered Wife," *Good Housekeeping*, p. 136.

33. Jennifer Baker Fleming, *Stopping Wife Abuse*, p. 83.

34. Del Martin, *Battered Wives*, p. 126.

35. *Congressional Record*. Washington, D.C. August 25, 1980.

36. For this claim that affluent women are economically trapped, see Lisa Leghorn, "Working With Battered Women," p. 97; Susan Schechter, *Women and Male Violence*, p. 237; "Battered Women," *Essence*.

37. Claims-makers often argue that a battered woman type of person feels humiliated and embarrassed and therefore is hesitant to tell her troubles to others. See Lenore Walker, *The Battered Woman*, for claims that men often inflict isolation as a means of control; see Dee L. R. Graham et. al., "Survivors of Terror," for claims that such isolation leads a battered woman to develop characteristics typical of long-term political hostages. Claims about the non-responsiveness of informal networks of assistance run throughout. See R. Emerson Dobash and Russell P. Dobash, *Violence Against Wives*, for a chapter on "Relatives, Friends, and Neighbors."

38. Anne Flitcraft, "Testimony," p. 193. Almost all claims-makers paint this image of the battered woman as a woman who should expect no help from formal agencies of assistance. See, for example, the United States Commission on Civil Rights, *Battered Women*, p. 20-97; and Del Martin's, *Battered Wives*, chapter on "Social Services, the Big Run Around." For sophisticated treatments of medical responses to such a woman see Evan Stark, et. al., "Medicine and Patriarchal Violence"; and Demie Kurz and Evan Stark, "Not-So-Benign Neglect."

39. "He Beat Me," *Vogue*, p. 186.

40. Such traditionally feminine attitudes associated with the battered woman appear throughout. See, for example, Del Martin, "What Keeps a Woman Captive"; R. Emerson and Russell P. Dobash, *Violence Against Wives*, particularly the chapter on how the girl is "prepared"; Elizabeth Truninger,

"Marital Violence"; and "If you Loved Me," *Redbook*, p. 104.

41. This robot image of woman's socialization also is common. See Marta Segovia-Ashley, "Shelters"; "Curbing the Wife-Beaters," *Macleans*, p. 41; "Battered Women," *Ebony*, p. 98; "Battered Women," *Essence*, p. 126.

42. Patricia G. Ball and Elizabeth Wyman, "Battered Wives and Powerlessness," p. 546.

43. Jennifer Baker Fleming, *Stopping Wife Abuse*, p. 9. Explicitly constructing a battered woman as a feminist symbol of what is wrong is powerful. "Wife Abuse," *Christianity Today*, p. 23 declared "frankly, the subject of wife abuse is a persuasive argument for feminism."

44. Jeannie Niedemeyer, "Testimony," p. 176; and Judge Golden Johnson, "Testimony," p. 61. These testimonies make such explicit claims in public policy hearings. See also Kathleen Tierney, "The Battered Women Movement," p. 215.

45. Judge Lisa Richette, "Testimony," p. 131; Del Martin, *Battered Wives*, p. 76; Mildred Daly Pagelow, *Family Violence*, p. 307; *Final Report*, Attorney General's Task Force, p. 3. Each claim that the battered woman is generally fearful.

46. Susan V. McLeer, "The Role of," p. 1158; Kay Lieberknecht, "Helping the Battered Wife"; "How to Recognize," *Glamour*, p. 206; "I Don't Want," *Ladies Home Journal*, p. 18. Each construct the battered woman as confused. In general, this theme runs throughout all claims. Likewise, the claim that a battered woman *is* angry appears throughout. See Dee L. R. Graham et. al., "Survivors of Terror," p. 230; Susan F. Turner and Constance Shapiro, "Battered Women"; Carol Nadelson and Maria Sauzier, "Intervention Programs," p. 157.

47. That a battered woman is characterized by a "negative self-image" is simply taken-for-granted: Dee L. R. Graham et. al., "Survivors of Terror," p. 229; Jillian Ridington, "The Transition Process," p. 568; Jennifer Baker Fleming, *Stopping Wife Abuse*, p. 85; "Why Women Stay," *Essence*, p. 147; "How Battered Women Can Get Help," *Readers Digest*, p. 21-23; "I Don't Want," *Ladies Home Journal*, p. 18; Dorie Klein, "Can This Marriage," p. 27; Carol Nadelson and Maria Sauzier, "Intervention Programs"; Elaine Hilberman and Kit Munson, "Sixty Battered Women."

48. This claim about physical and psychological illness most often is

implicit in the personal stories labeled as those of the battered woman where troubles clearly begin *after* victimization. For explicit claims see Anne Flitcraft, "Testimony a," p. 240; Elaine Hilberman and Kit Munson, "Sixty Battered Women"; and Dorie Klein, "Can This Marriage."

49. For such unflattering constructions see Margaret Ball, "Issues of Violence"; Patricia G. Ball and Elizabeth Wyman, "Battered Wives"; Elaine Hilberman and Kit Munson, "Sixty Battered Women"; and Jerry Finn, "The Stresses and Coping Behavior."

50. Betsy Warrior, *Working on Wife Abuse*, p. 1. Also, John M. Johnson, "Program Enterprise"; and Trova Hutchins and Vee Baxter, "Battered Women," examine the philosophical and organizational differences among shelters and advance claims that shelters associated with the modern problem called "wife abuse" neither treat women as the problem nor do they seek to save families.

51. For such descriptions of shelters and shelter clients see Del Martin, *Battered Wives*, p. 126; Lenore Walker, *The Battered Woman*, p. 202; Val Binney, et. al., "Refuges and Housing," p. 169-173; *Congressional Record* for August 25, 1980; "Shelters for Battered Wives," *McCalls*, p. 51; "London," *Ms.*, p. 24.

52. Lenore Walker, *The Battered Woman*, p. 198. This book claims "as soon as battered women walk through the door, they are no longer helpless victims"; Kathleen Ferraro, "Processing Battered Women," p. 436 argues "when women entered the shelter they were declaring independence from their husbands and extended families"; Betsy Warrior, *Working on Wife Abuse*, p. 73 argues a "woman coming to a shelter has already actually made the decision to leave her husband."

53. Shelly Fernandez, "Testimony," p. 117. For this claim that shelter clients are women with multiple problems see also Jillian Ridington, "The Transition Process," p. 567-569.

54. This is typical in social problem construction. Public problems are defined, solutions are proposed, and then the practical tasks of carrying out policy become the province of specialists. See, for example, Michael Lipsky, *Street-Level Bureaucracy*.

55. See Trova Hutchins and Vee Baxter, "Battered Women"; and Lisa Leghorn, "Working with Battered Women," for claims distinguishing shelters from emergency hotels.

56. See R. Emerson and Russell P. Dobash, *Violence Against Wives*, p. 225; Marta Segovia-Ashley, "Testimony," p. 101 for claims that shelters are places where a woman's right to self-determination is critical. At the same time, Trudy Mills and Sherryl Kleinman, "Emotions, Reflexivity and Action," p. 1019; Betsy Warrior, *Working on Wife Abuse*, p. 72; Colleen McGrath, "The Crisis of Domestic Order," p. 26; and Elizabeth Schillinger, "Dependency, Control, and Isolation" argue that shelters have one service goal: to encourage a woman's independence. Thus, Trova Hutchins and Vee Baxter, "Battered Women," note that nearly all shelters discourage contact with men.

57. Betsy Warrior, *Working on Wife Abuse*, p. 73.

58. Trova Hutchins and Vee Baxter, "Battered Women"; Jenny Clifton, "Refuges and Self-Help," p. 41.

59. For claims that shelters attempt to "re-socialize" their clients see Jillian Ridington, "The Transition Process," p. 569; "Shelters for Battered Wives," *McCalls*, p. 51. This goal of resocialization can be stated more forcefully. Mary Romero, "A Comparison Between Strategies," p. 545 claims victims need first to be "deprogrammed" before they are "resocialized to feminist values."

60. Gail Sullivan and Jane Weiss, "How We Support Battered Women"; and Elizabeth Schillinger, "Dependency, Control, and Isolation" argue this theme of no professionals or experts. Patricia A. Morgan, "Constructing Images of Deviance," examines the meaning of professionalization in macro-political terms.

61. Quoted in Susan Schechter, *Women and Male Violence*, p. 67.

62. These are the two major themes describing how women victims should change their personal attitudes. According to claims, to become a "not-battered" woman, a woman must focus on her anger and reject self-blame. See Kathleen J. Ferraro and John M. Johnson, "How Women Experience Battering." But this does not mean a woman requires psychological "therapy." Shelters identified with the modern-day problem of wife abuse began with a distinctly anti-therapy model of social service provision. See Marta Segoaia-Ashley, "Shelters," p. 385; and Elizabeth Schillinger, "Dependency, Control, and Isolation."

63. This is a construction of shelters as social movement organizations. Such places offer social services *and* engage in political action to change the social order. Not surprisingly, there are continuing debates among shelter insiders about the proper mix of service and politics. Also, as social movement orga-

nizations, shelters often are judged as much by *how* they are organized as by *what* they accomplish. Of course, such debates are not a part of mass media claims about shelters, and the discussion of shelters as social movement organizations rarely enters public policy hearings where the issue is narrowly formulated as one of providing services to victims and where discussion of feminist political action might hurt chances of securing public money and support. Since my interest is in *public* collective representations, I will not pursue an analysis of shelters as social movement organizations. But one point is clear: What is deemed good for the battered woman type of person is a shelter organized as a social movement organization. Each characteristic associated with such organizations has been translated into claims about the needs of the battered woman. So, readers do not need to know that social movement organizations, in general, advocate participatory democracy, self-determination, and so on. For constructions of shelters as social movement organizations see Gail Sullivan, "Cooptation"; Barbara J. Hart, "Burn-Out"; Colleen McGrath, "The Crisis of Domestic Order."

64. Jillian Ridington, "The Transition Process," p. 569.

65. Anne Flitcraft, "Testimony b," p. 114. A shelter, in other words, provides not only an escape *from* abuse but also an escape *to* a community.

66. Susan Schechter, *Women and Male Violence*, p. 60, for example, claims "although there is rapid turnover in residents, relationships among women form quickly, based on similar experiences, common living spaces, and the necessity of accomplishing major tasks. Mildred Daly Pagelow, *Woman-Battering*, p. 158 argues: "It takes only a short time for most women to realize that other women have had the same experiences and felt basically the same emotions."

67. Lisa Leghorn, quoted in Jennifer Baker Fleming, *Stopping Wife Abuse*, p. 30.

68. Jenny Clifton, "Refuges and Self Help," p. 41. Self-help, called the "fundamental principle of organization," is explicitly contrasted with "therapeutic models" of service provision. See also Carol S. Wharton, "Splintered Visions," p. 53-54.

69. Jillian Ridington, "The Transition Process," p. 572.

70. Betsy Warrior, *Working on Wife Abuse*, p. 91.

71. For the ambiguous role of shelter workers see Jenny Clifton, "Refuges

and Self Help," p. 44. The over emphasis on assisting clients is associated with claims constructing several types of negative outcomes. For example, doing "too much" for clients leads to worker "burn-out" because workers find they cannot do everything; it promotes workers taking power away from clients; it discourages clients from learning the skills needed for independent living. For claims about workers in shelters also see Susan Schechter, *Women and Male Violence*; Gail Sullivan, "Cooptation"; Barbara J. Hart, "Burn-Out"; Noelie Rodriguez, "Transcending Bureaucracy."

72. R. Emerson and Russell P. Dobash, *Violence Against Wives*, p. 225.

73. Monica Erler, Testimony," p. 113. Within this prescriptive set of claims about what shelters should do and how they should do it, accomplishing service goals often seems automatic. Lenore Walker, *The Battered Woman*, p. 198-199, claims: "Battered women come to a shelter or safe house terrified of their future. By the time they are ready to leave, they generally have confidence they can make it alone."

74. See Lenore Walker, *The Battered Woman*, p. 202; Erin Pizzey, "Pizzey Comments"; "London," *Ms.*, p. 24 for such constructions of the battered woman as a grateful client who does not mind the dismal nature of the shelter environment.

75. See Mildred Daly Pagelow, *Woman-Battering*, p. 158 for such constructions of shelter clients as women who will somewhat automatically form a cohesive community. Pagelow argues "class, racial, and ethnic differences that keep most women divided all but disappear inside shelters"; and "It takes only a short time for most women to realize that other women have the same experiences and felt the same emotions." Susan Schechter, *Women and Male Violence*, p. 60 also argues that inside shelters "relationships form quickly based on similar experiences, common living space and the sharing of food and coffee." Although there are many warnings about the necessity of keeping racism and classism out of shelters, the image is that problems are somewhat easily resolvable since "tension dissipates at house meetings." (Susan Schechter, *Women and Male Violence*, p. 61.) The major point here is that within the collective image of shelters, clients are known only as each is an instance of the battered woman type of person and this circumvents the logical prediction that a cooperative, therapeutic environment would be unlikely given member transience and differences among women sharing living space.

Chapter 2

1. Gale Miller and James A. Holstein, "On the Sociology of Social Problems," p. 5.

2. During a public policy hearing, this comment was made by James H. Scheuer, "Comment," p. 147. It was in response to Lenore Walker's attempt to include vaguely defined "emotional abuse" within the content of "wife abuse."

3. See, for example, Monica Blumenthal, et. al., *Justifying Violence*, for a study on the attitudes of American men about violence in general; Richard J. Gelles and Murray A. Straus, "Determinants of Violence," p. 554-560, for conceptual distinctions between violence and force, aggression and assertion, legitimate and illegitimate violence and between instrumental and expressive violence. Val Borkowski and her colleagues, *Marital Violence*, have studied the working definitions of "marital violence" held by several types of social service providers.

4. Child abuse claims-makers have given much attention to this issue of differences between child abuse and "parental punishment" no doubt because mandatory reporting laws raise the practical question of diagnosis. See, for example, Jeanne M. Giovannoni and Rosina M. Becerra, *Defining Child Abuse*; Richard O'Toole, et. al., "Theories"; and Sharon P. Herzberger and Howard Tennen, "The Effect of Self-Relevance." These illustrate complexities similar to those of evaluating differences between "wife abuse" and "normal marital violence."

5. The commonly used, but often criticized, Conflict Tactics Scale (Murray A. Straus, et. al., *Behind Closed Doors*), labels as "abusive violence" those acts having a high potential for injuring the person being hit. This rule for evaluating the moral meaning of violence is more complicated than I am stating. According to Cathy Greenblatt, "A Hit is a Hit," the rule also is gendered since she found more tolerance of a wife slapping her husband than for a husband slapping his wife. But this evaluative difference is supported by the same probability reasoning—a woman will likely not do as much damage with a "slap" as a man will. Therefore, this rule forgiving women's violence holds only for seemingly minimal violence. A woman who engages in extreme sounding violence receives *more* condemnation than does a man. See Ann Jones, *Women Who Kill*, for this examination in relation to women who kill their partners.

6. Debra Kalmuss, "The Attribution of Responsibility," found this attention

to injuries in studies using vignettes. As another example, this is legal precedent in New York State Law where assault in the third degree is "intentionally causing injury"; assault in the second degree is "intentionally causing serious injury"; assault in the first degree is "intentionally disfiguring another person seriously, or intentionally destroying, amputating or permanently disabling a member or organ."

7. See for example, Michele Bograd, "Feminist Perspectives"; and Andrea Sedlak, "The Effects of Personal Experiences."

8. Cathy Greenblatt, "A Hit is a Hit"; Andrea Sedlak, "The Effects of Personal Experiences"; Deborah Richardson and Jennifer L. Campbell, "Alcohol and Wife Abuse." This notion of "worthiness" in the use of violence also can be an assessment of victim "respectability." A victim judged as not a respectable type of person simultaneously is judged as "deserving" violence.

9. This claim that wife abuse is not judged by the same criteria as other assault is most explicit when claims-makers argue that the criminal justice system should treat it as a "regular crime." See *Final Report*, Attorney General's Task Force; Laurie Wermuth, "Domestic Violence." Thus, claims-makers argue "as a class, battered women are denied the protection accorded to other victims of crime" (Marjory Fields, "Testimony," p. 21).

10. Candace Clark, "Sympathy Biography." Clark also argues that sympathy entitlement varies by social status. A woman, for example, might claim more sympathy for car trouble than a man because evaluators anticipate men have the skills to resolve the situation themselves; children elicit more sympathy than do adults, and so on. While such rules apply to the interpersonal process of sympathy exchange, they do not seem relevant to this discussion about sympathy associated with *social types*. All that is deemed relevant about the battered woman type of person is contained within the collective representation and that is homogeneous. However, I will return to this when I discuss sympathy within a shelter for the battered woman. Since such places serve individual women, the interpersonal dimensions of sympathy exchange become relevant.

11. Robert M. Bellah et. al., *Habits of the Heart*, p. 20. According to Bellah and his colleagues, individualism is a common moral vocabulary used by Americans to make sense of our public and private lives. According to Alex de Tocqueville, "Of Individualism in Democracies," p. 508, when we organize the world in these terms, we ". . . owe no man anything and hardly expect anything

from anybody. (We) form the habit of thinking of ourselves in isolation and imagine that our whole destiny is in our own hands." Within this vocabulary, individual responsibility is highly valued, social structural constraints are denied.

12. See chapter 1 for discussion and references on such constructions.

13. Certainly this collective representation *did* change notions of the sympathy worthiness of the battered woman *type of person*. Prior to the 1970s, the general construction was that a woman who was assaulted caused it and/or liked it; her behavior of staying was understood as reflecting her choice. This interrelated system of cultural interpretations supported the public stance that such a woman did not need nor did she deserve public sympathy.

14. Alfred Schutz, *Collected Papers*, Vol. 1, part 1.

15. I saw this in a court case involving a woman who had been "slapped." She lost her balance and fell back, hitting her head on a bookcase, which came down on her yielding permanent and severe injury. The judge ruled the injury was "accidental."

16. Although researchers attempting to discover the rules for the moral evaluation of violence often use sophisticated multiple regression statistical techniques enabling them to assess several contingencies simultaneously, there are always further rules to be discovered. Moreover, claims-makers sometimes argue that evaluations of violence also depend on the characteristics of *evaluators*. For general differences in evaluation, see Peter H. Rossi et. al., "The Seriousness of Crimes"; and Monica Blumenthal, et. al., *Justifying Violence*. In addition, Deborah Richardson and Jennifer L. Campbell, "Alcohol and Wife Abuse" found in a vignette experiment that women blamed men more than men blamed men; Debra Kalmuss, "The Attribution of Responsibility," on the other hand, found in vignette experiments women subjects did not assign less responsibility to the wife as compared with men subjects. Likewise, Sharon P. Herzberger and Howard Tennen, "The Effect of Self-Relevance," found evaluations of child abuse depended on personal experiences with parental violence while Cathy Greenblatt, "A Hit is a Hit," found no such relationship. It seems safe to claim that the search for sources of differences in the moral evaluation of violence is an endless task, for evaluations will be made only situationally.

17. Eli H. Newberger, "The Helping Hand"; and Richard O'Toole and his colleagues, "Theories," found that in the professional diagnosis of child abuse commonsense reasoning led to "social class" and "race" becoming primary

indicators. In other words, what is and what is not evaluated as child abuse depends on characteristics independent of the behavior. See also Val Borkowski and her colleagues, *Marital Violence* (chapter 4), for further evidence supporting my claim that professionals use the same criteria as do lay evaluators in diagnosing wife abuse.

18. For examples of reinterpretations of a woman's definitions to fit what would be expected of a battered woman type of person see Elizabeth A. Waites, "Female Masochism," p. 542. Waites argues the "statement that abused wives love their abusers need not be taken at face value. It may represent merely a denial of ambivalence or even unmitigated hatred." Natalie Shainess, "Psychological Aspects," p. 118 claims the "only reasons the woman does not end the marriage are dependence—emotional or practical—and fear of change and the unknown. These are often masked as love or so the woman deludes herself."

19. Bonnie Lewis, "The Wife Abuse Inventory"; or John S. Brekke, "Detecting Wife Abuse." These works state explicit formulations of what to look for in order to diagnose a battered woman.

20. Lenore Walker, *The Battered Woman*, p. 31. This particular list has very real consequences because it is used in legal proceedings for the "battered woman's defense." Such a defense is used when a woman kills her husband in other than immediate self-defense. *If* a woman seemingly fits this profile of a "battered woman" and *if* her relationship seemingly fits the profile of an "abusive relationship," then she can be found not guilty of murder.

21. Harold Garfinkel, *Studies in Ethnomethodology*, p. 76-103.

Chapter 3

1. Observers of most shelters often claim such places do *not* even remotely resemble their collective representation. Within these arguments, shelters are understood as instances of social movement organizations experiencing the typical problems of transformation and cooptation. See, for example, John M. Johnson, "Program Enterprise"; Patricia A. Morgan, "Constructing Images"; Gail Sullivan, "Cooptation," for general descriptions of this process in shelters. Also see Lois Ahrens, "Battered Women's Refuges," for a specifically feminist criticism of this process. Kathleen Ferraro, "Processing Battered Women," and "Negotiating Trouble," has used this social movement framework to examine one such ongoing organization.

2. Actually, there were two shelters in this county managed by the FVP. My original plan was to collect data from both, but I gave up quite quickly when initial observation showed the two places to be very different. Consider, as one example, the myriad practical consequences of the "size of the local community." While South Coast was in a medium-sized city, the other shelter was in a small town. Clients in the small town shelter often were not strangers either to workers or to one another. South Coast clients rarely knew one another or workers before they entered. Also, while rents in the small town were lower, making it easier to move clients from the shelter, there were fewer employment opportunities, making it more difficult for clients to find jobs. Furthermore, the supporting social service networks in the small town were not well-developed, but the local churches were more supportive. In brief, a detailed analysis of the context of social problems work in formal agencies is necessary for this work always is situated.

3. While there was a funding requirement that services were available only to county residents, all workers agreed it was not sensible. A battered woman often needs to leave her local community and, therefore, it is important for shelters to establish ties with other such places. Sending clients elsewhere requires reciprocity and South Coast often took in women from other counties and states. However, the rule did serve as a convenient worker resource when they did not want to do this. A woman calling from another place could be told, "Sorry, it's the rule; we can take only county residents."

4. In this way, South Coast seems very different from the shelter studied by Kathleen Ferraro, "Processing Battered Women," and "Negotiating Trouble," where the *focus* seemed to be on counseling clients. It is true that some South Coast workers, particularly those who themselves were in therapy, could be inclined to "encourage" clients to "see a counselor." But this was not the formal model of shelter work at this place.

5. Rules justified as necessary for clients' safety also were justified as necessary for *workers'* safety. There was a constant circulation of stories at South Coast about vaguely defined "other shelters" where confidentiality had been broken, allowing angry batterers to locate the shelter and kill both clients and workers. See Carol Wharton's, "Splintered Visions" analysis of this "state of sieze" mentality of shelter workers.

6. Asking clients to be responsible for the organization most often involved the troublesome "third shift," from midnight to eight in the morning. Regardless

of the popular image, most women called and entered South Coast during the day and evening hours. On a typical night, the on duty worker would have eight hours of sleep so it was difficult to justify the presence of a paid staff member. But the phone *could* ring, and there *could* be an emergency. The organization repeatedly tried to implement a plan whereby one or another client would sleep in the downstairs private room and answer the phone should it ring and merely route any calls to a backup worker who would take care of it. But the plan never worked because clients simply refused to do this for the organization. Some women said they felt incapable of handling such a responsibility, others refused saying they did not want to do this.

Chapter 4

1. James A. Holstein, "Mental Illness." Michael Lipsky, *Street-Level Bureaucracy*, also argues that secretaries and receptionists informally perform the same screening functions for social service workers. At South Coast, workers themselves answered all calls.

2. In this section examining what workers said about "appropriateness," I will primarily be using data from formal interviews that are explained in the appendix.

3. Although not particularly common, from time to time former clients, who knew the location of this place and who experienced problems, would simply appear at the door. Also from time to time, workers would receive a call from the police who already had helped a woman leave her home.

4. Within the collective representation of the battered woman, it seems not possible that a woman would choose to not enter a shelter, yet this was quite common at South Coast. The justifications for women's decisions to not enter are too diverse to enumerate but I will give examples: Some women wanted private accommodations and objected to the communal living arrangement. From time to time there were outbreaks of infectious diseases and prospective clients would not want to chance infection; some women made unacceptable demands (i.e. one woman wanted a guarantee that workers would be always available to baby-sit her children; another woman demanded that the shelter store her entire household of furniture). Other women declined entry when they learned they would be responsible for their share of communal housekeeping chores, or when they heard there was mandatory participation in support groups.

5. This problem of faulty information remained when clients were referred by area social service providers. According to workers, these persons, too, could be somewhat less than truthful in their efforts to secure housing for their clients.

6. Kathleen Ferraro, "Processing Battered Women," p. 423 has noted this hesitancy about client selection decisions for workers at another shelter. Data she presented best conveys this worker hesitation:

> I'm still sketchy about who we take in and who we don't. Like, O.K., one case I was telling you about today, you know, she's marginally acceptable, *maybe*, you know, I don't know, maybe she is, maybe she isn't . . . and we do have space, or we will.

7. See the appendix for information on the shelter log, the worker written running commentary on life inside South Coast. I repeat here that I will maintain confidentiality. Thus, I have changed names and anything else that might identify individual women. The number at the end of each log segment shows the day on which the entry appeared.

8. The example of Margaret at the beginning of this section demonstrates the same point. According to that note, the worker told Margaret that South Coast dealt only with emergency physical abuse, but this formal justification was located within a second—this woman wanted shelter only for one night.

9. To give only a few examples, the "battered woman" gestalt could be created by constructing the petitioner as a woman who had been labeled as "battered" by others and as a "fearful woman" who had experienced long-term brutal assault:

> Call from policeman saying he had a badly battered woman. She is afraid of husband finding her. He has been violent to her all during their four-year marriage, has shot at her and held a butcher knife to her throat. Went to pick her up.
>
> [655]

A battered woman gestalt could be created by constructing a petitioner as a woman recently victimized, as a woman experiencing psychological problems from abuse, one who had made repeated efforts to remove herself from her abuse, and one whose victimization was bad enough to involve law enforcement:

> Call from Gloria. She had just been very beat up and requested shelter. Met her and

brought her in—a very classical case and nice woman. I really enjoyed talking to her, she's pretty hip to the psychological trips. She was at the shelter two years ago, this time the police took him away.

[591]

Or, a battered woman gestalt could be created simply by constructing the petitioner as an oppressed woman who displayed the subjectivity of a battered woman:

... She seems like a classic battered case. Had a long session with her, she was crying and very hurt. Absolutely no self-esteem, husband treated her like a child but she is still in love with him. ... She feels very helpless and lonely.

[343]

Conversely, a "not-battered" gestalt could be created by constructing a woman as one not wanting services and as offering no history of abuse:

Call from woman, wouldn't give name. Needed place to stay. Doubtful whether she's battered, wouldn't talk about past battery situations so couldn't discern eligibility.

[821]

Or, a "not-battered" gestalt could be created by constructing the petitioner's *partner* as not an "abusive man," and by constructing the violence as not "wife abuse:"

Kathy is a very sweet girl, not able to cope with separation from her husband, he only eighteen years old, working long hours daily (15), returns from work tired, Kathy has been alone all day caring for baby, in need of companion, husband gets angry if child cries or Kathy is upset at anything. She says she loves her husband and "deep down" doesn't want to break up. Her description of their quarrels doesn't sound like a battered situation.

[693]

Or, a "not-battered" gestalt could be created by constructing the woman as one with the "wrong attitude" and the "wrong demeanor" for a "battered woman:"

Crisis call from Daniele, extremely young woman with "ruff attitude"—if he hits me I always hit him back—referred to [another shelter].

[410]

Or, a "not-battered" gestalt could be created by constructing a petitioner as a woman not in a typical situation of wife abuse:

Crisis call from woman who has hitchhiked with male who has since left. On welfare, but can't afford hotels anymore. When I mentioned that this was a shelter for battered women, she started reaching to qualify.

[836]

I offer these examples to support my point: There was no list of characteristics necessary or sufficient to construct a "battered woman" or a "not-battered woman" gestalt.

10. C. Wright Mills, "Situated Actions." See also Kathleen Ferraro, "Processing Battered Women" for an example of workers' use of "vibes" as a method to account for selection decisions in another shelter.

11. There were only a few times when a log entry would give more of the folk reasoning grounds upon which a label of "inappropriate client" rested. For example:

> Crisis call from Amy—she was talking so fast that I could barely understand. She said she needed shelter because someone she knows is beating her. She sounded real spacey—I suggested friends, relatives. She said everybody hates her. I followed my instincts and said we were full.
>
> [633]

Or:

> Toni called twice, says her husband threatened to throw her out at midnight. She sounds dippy to me but states she is a verbally abused woman. . . . She really sounds like a strange woman, I think she is looking for a shoulder to cry on.
>
> [763]

Chapter 5

1. Shelter records for 11/159 clients contained a notation that the woman had been "kicked out" of her home by her partner. Another new client said she had been living in a motel with her partner. After he assaulted her, he left and refused to pay further room charges. Not much can be made of these numbers since they were taken from client information forms where there was no specific question asked about whether or not a woman had "chosen" to leave her home.

2. In one particular instance, a worker at Child Protective Services apparently told a woman "either you leave your abusive husband or I will remove your children from your home." Many clients were referred by other local social services, but I do not know how often such referrals resulted in a client who was not truly "voluntary."

3. As South Coast's relationships with local police strengthened, this situation worsened. Police in the area did arrest abusers but there still were some instances where a woman refused to sign a citizen's arrest form, where the woman and her partner told conflicting stories, and where there was not enough evidence of assault to justify arrest. Police who nonetheless feared further violence (and therefore further calls for assistance) sometimes resolved the situation by contacting South Coast. For example, police called me one night at 2:00 A.M. They already had taken a woman and her baby to an all night restaurant in lieu of arresting both the woman and her partner—not sensible since then the baby would need placement in a foster home. This woman told me she had become angry at her husband for his failure to economically provide and she had threatened him with a kitchen knife. He then beat her up. While she perhaps was not a classic exemplar of a battered woman, I did take her to South Coast without hesitation because I could see no alternative.

4. This seems typical of ongoing shelters. See Trudy Mills and Sherryl Kleinman, "Emotions, Reflexivity and Action"; and Susan B. Murray, "The Unhappy Marriage," for examples of shelters where Lenore Walker's, *The Battered Woman*, "cycle of violence" theory has become the dominant worker interpretive device.

5. See chapter 3 for more discussion of the logic of these rules.

6. Peter L. Berger and Thomas Luckmann, *The Social Construction of Reality*.

7. These implicit and explicit rules at South Coast seem typical of most ongoing shelters sharing the goal of transforming the battered woman. While each place differs, other shelters seemingly have even greater structural supports for achieving this identity transformation. For example, it seems not uncommon for such places to have rules absolutely prohibiting a client from contacting her partner, or rules prohibiting such contact except in the presence of a shelter worker. Such rules, of course, prohibit contact with the person most likely to reconfirm a client's old identity. Furthermore, although South Coast did have a curfew that limited clients' time with outsiders, this always was set somewhere between 10:00 P.M. and 1:00 A.M. In contrast, it is not atypical for shelters to set curfews at dusk, which would be even more limiting. Still further, while South Coast officially only encouraged clients to arrange formal counseling sessions, other shelters mandate this and thus ensure that clients receive large doses of organizationally approved plausibility structures. South Coast, in

brief, seems more-or-less typical of other such places where organizational structures not surprisingly are in the service of organizational goals. Most of my references here are unpublished or available only to shelter movement insiders. But see Carol Wharton, "Splintered Visions"; Susan B. Murray, "The Unhappy Marriage"; and Elizabeth Schillinger, "Dependency, Control and Isolation" for descriptions of other shelters.

8. For example:

Talked with Jane about her feelings like she is being dissected by the staff. . . . She would like it if staff would ask her how she's feeling rather than assuming or labeling her.

[414]

9. Carol Wharton, "Splintered Visions" argues that workers at another shelter focused exclusively on the *anger* that should be experienced by a battered woman. South Coast workers also believed that *sadness* was an appropriate emotion. For a more complete examination of the emotions work assumed to be needed by the battered woman type of person see Trudy Mills and Sherryl Kleinmann, "Emotions, Reflexivity and Action."

10. Susan B. Murray, "The Unhappy Marriage" noted this same dynamic at another shelter where workers were most concerned with transforming clients' subjective identities while clients themselves were most concerned with practical needs.

11. Again, this seems not all that atypical of shelters in general. For example, Kathleen Ferraro, "Processing Battered Women," found workers at one such place were focused on clients' perceived needs for counseling; Susan B. Murray, "The Unhappy Marriage," found workers at another such place were most concerned with teaching clients how to define themselves in terms of the "cycle of violence" theory. Other examinations of this tension in shelter work, however, differ from mine. That is, both Ferraro and Murray claim the focus on clients' subjective identities was not within original feminist-identified constructions of the battered woman type of person. I disagree and argue that while there definitely *are* practical considerations encouraging workers to focus on clients' subjectivities (i.e. the relative glamour of counseling activities in modern-day America, the often impossible task of obtaining material resources to change women's material lives), the construction of the battered woman as a woman *needing* subjective identity transformation is at the core of the collective representation of this type of woman. Stated otherwise, claims constructed the

battered woman type of person as a woman who would *automatically* achieve
subjective identity transformation within shelters. In practice, such a transformation is not always automatic, and hence, it becomes something to be accomplished by social service providers.

12. Clearly, these workers were not mere rule enforcers. Workers often suspended rules in order to achieve the intent of rules. In one case, for example, a
rule was constructed as hindering a client from discarding her old identity and
this explicitly justified rule suspension:

> Erma wanted to know if it was OK for her to go to the beach with her kids even
> though her 72-hours is not up. She said . . . she is spending too much time dwelling
> on her husband. I said it was all right due to the circumstances.
>
> [721]

13. Again, I use the insights of Peter Berger and Thomas Luckmann, *The
Social Construction of Reality*, p. 159. In this work, Berger and Luckmann
argue it is not sufficient to merely "discount" old identities; they must be com-
pletely "annihilated" if the process of identity transformation is to be successful.
Certainly the social construction of the "abusive man" contains the interpretations necessary to accomplish such an annihilation.

14. I put "free" in quotes to call attention to its ambiguity. Yes, a client
could simply leave this place. The worst thing that could happen would be that
workers would decide she was not eligible to enter again. Yet *free* implies
choice and many clients did not have such a choice. If they left South Coast,
they would have no where else to go. Thus, the same conditions trapping
women in abusive relationships could trap them in this shelter.

15. In one instance, support was very tangible—workers loaned money to
a client, something rarely done since money was the most scarce resource at
this place. But in that instance, the loan seemingly was justified as a reward for
acting in organizationally approved ways:

> Robbie needs money, has no food. We may want to loan her a bit till welfare comes
> through. She's really holding her ground with her husband—I can't believe how
> strong and clearly she's thinking. It will be great to keep supporting this.
>
> [785]

16. This compression of people into the categories of "battered woman"
and "abusive man" obviously is not limited to South Coast. Mildred Daly
Pagelow, *Woman-Battering*, p. 158 reports on another shelter where, during a
group discussion, one client said, "It sounds like we're all talking about the

same man." Certainly this belief that all clients' husbands were the same is made possible by focusing on each man only as he is an instance of an abusive man.

17. Michael Lipsky, *Street-Level* Bureaucracy.

Chapter 6

1. Kathleen Ferraro, "Negotiating Trouble," p. 432 makes this same point: By focusing on the violence, shelter workers learn only about "isolated fragments" of their clients' lives.

2. See chapter 1 for such glowing reports about the tranquility of life inside shelters.

3. With one exception (Noelie Rodriguez, "Transcending Bureaucracy") observers have focused on criticizing such places for not putting social movement ideals into practice. See the work of Kathleen Ferraro, "Negotiating Trouble," and "Processing Battered Women"; Kathleen Ferraro and John M. Johnson, "How Women Experience"; and Carol Wharton, "Splintered Visions." Such examinations, of course, assume practical experiences *can* and *should* match collective representations.

4. The most common type of trouble was associated with the inability of clients to talk with one another. Spanish-speaking women often found themselves alone and isolated in the shelter and unable to communicate with English-speaking clients and workers.

5. My numbers are quite vague and I cannot say much about these clients. The tendency was for workers to simply *erase* them from the records and from talk immediately following exit. The only record for most of these women was on the "ineligible list" where workers would note women deemed *inappropriate* for South Coast services. But even here, rarely did workers say *why* they labeled a client as "inappropriate."

6. Of course, if these workers were social movement activists they might see their efforts as part of a larger cause. But only one shelter coordinator at South Coast constructed the meaning of her work in this way. She said:

> I feel like this has been an ongoing struggle and will continue to be an ongoing struggle and that working on issues of battered women are the crux of what needs to happen for women to be not the most shit-upon person in the world. If we can

solve the battered woman problem, which will never happen in our lifetime, then maybe all women's problems will be solved. Because she seems to be the core of what's happening as a result of inequality and sexism.

7. Again, for my discussion of the social rules for sympathy giving and getting, I am relying on the work of Candace Clark, "Sympathy Biography."

8. For an example of this tendency to deflect troubles back onto clients in other types of social service organizations see David R. Buckholt and Jaber F. Gubrium, "Practicing Accountability."

9. Compare this note with the previous example where a woman came back late and "smelled of booze" *because* she was a battered woman type of person. In that instance, the woman was not evicted and the rule violation was constructed as yielding a "good experience" for her. Here the client was constructed as a "not-battered woman" and she *was* evicted from this place for breaking the same two rules.

10. The reasons for losing contact with former clients who were perhaps "successful" are common sense. Shelter residence marks a difficult time in a woman's life. If she manages to move on to something better, she might not want to be reminded of this time. And, just as simply, South Coast was a service organization. Just as few of us would contact our physician months after an illness to say, "I'm still feeling fine," successful clients had no reason to contact this place. I became intrigued with this issue of what happened to former clients quite early in my research and I tried to do a follow-up study. It was a miserable failure—I could not locate many former clients in the first place; many women were not happy with the idea that I wanted to contact them; women moved from place to place and I lost contact with them. Within two months, I was left with only a few women—those who treated me like a shelter worker and needed further service. I know of no follow-up studies of shelter residents that have managed to follow a significant number of these women for any length of time.

11. On this point, I am agreeing with Kathleen Ferraro, "Processing Battered Women" and "Negotiating Trouble." Ferraro has found that workers blame clients for service failures. But I am disagreeing with her claim that his is the result of a "therapeutic ideology" somehow external to the social problems claims constructing the battered woman type of person. While it might well be true that workers in both shelters constructed clients as "less than fully-competent" adults, workers at South Coast went one step further: They con-

structed their clients in these terms but then made sense of this construction in terms of the battered woman collective representation.

Chapter 7

1. Alfred Schutz, *Collected Papers*, Vol. 1.

2. Mary Douglas, *How Institutions Think.*

3. See, for example, John M. Johnson, "Horror Stories," for an examination of the formal properties of viable "child abuse" claims and the role of horror stories in achieving claim viability.

4. See Joel Best, "Dark Figures." This work is an examination of claims about missing children.

5. Candace Clark, "Sympathy Biography."

6. Alfred Schutz, *Collected Papers*, Vol. 1.

REFERENCES

————. 1979. "Projects, Programs and Shelters." *Aegis: Magazine on Ending Violence Against Women.* (January/February): 12.

Ahrens, Lois. 1980. "Battered Women's Refuges: Feminist Cooperatives vs. Social Service Institutions." *Aegis: Magazine on Ending Violence Against Women.* (Summer/Autumn): 9-15.

Attorney General's Task Force on Family Violence. 1984. *Final Report.* Washington, D.C.: U.S. Government Printing Office.

Bako, Yolanda. 1978. "Testimony." *Battered Women: Issues of Public Policy.* Washington, D.C. United States Commission on Civil Rights, 66-73.

Ball, Margaret. 1977. "Issues of Violence in Family Casework." *Social Casework* 58(1):3-12.

Ball, Patricia G., and Elizabeth Wyman. 1977/1978. "Battered Wives and Powerlessness: What Can Counselors Do?" *Victimology* 2(3,4):545-552.

Bass, David, and Janet Rice. 1979. "Agency Responses to the Abused Wife." *Social Casework* 60(6):338-342.

Bellah, Robert N.; Richard Madsen; William M. Sullivan; Ann Swidler, and Steven M. Tipton. 1985. *Habits of the Heart: Individualism and Commitment in American Life.* Berkeley: University of California Press.

Berger, Peter L., and Thomas Luckmann. 1967. *The Social Construction of Reality.* New York: Anchor Books.

Best, Joel. 1989. "Dark Figures and Child Victims: Statistical Claims about Missing Children." In *Images of Issues: Typifying Contemporary Social Problems*, edited by Joel Best, 21-37. New York: Aldine De Gruyter.

————. 1987. "Rhetoric in Claims-making: Constructing the Missing Children Problem." *Social Problems* 34(2):101-121.

Binney, Val, Gina Harkell, and Judy Nixon. 1985. "Refuges and Housing for Battered Women." In *Private Violence and Public Policy: The Needs of Battered Women and the Response of Public Services*, edited by Jan Pahl, 166-178. Boston: Routledge and Kegan Paul.

Blumenthal, Monica D., Robert L. Kahn, Frank M. Andrews, and Kendra B. Head. 1972. *Justifying Violence: Attitudes of American Men*. Ann Arbor, MI: Institute for Social Research.

Bograd, Michele. 1988. "Feminist Perspectives on Wife Abuse: An Introduction." In *Feminist Perspectives on Wife Abuse*, edited by Kersti Yllö and Michele Bograd, 11-26. Beverly Hills: Sage Publications.

——— . 1984. "Family Systems Approaches to Wife Battering: A Feminist Critique." *American Journal of Orthopsychiatry* 54(4):558-568.

Borkowski, Margaret; Mervyn Murch, and Val Walker. 1983. *Marital Violence: The Community Response*. New York: Tavistock.

Brekke, John S. 1987. "Detecting Wife and Child Abuse in Clinical Settings." *Social Casework* 68(6):332-338.

Breines, Wini, and Linda Gordon. 1983. "The New Scholarship on Family Violence." *Signs* 8(3):490-531.

Buckholdt, David R., and Jaber F. Gubrium. 1983. "Practicing Accountability in Human Service Organizations." *Urban Life* 12(3):249-268.

Christianity Today.
    1983. "Wife Abuse: The Silent Crime" (K. W. Peterson). Nov. 25:22-26.

Clark, Candace. 1987. "Sympathy Biography and Sympathy Margin." *American Journal of Sociology* 93(2):290-321.

Clifton, Jenny. 1985. "Refuges and Self-Help." In *Marital Violence*, edited by Norman Johnson, 40-59. Boston: Routledge and Kegan Paul.

Clinch, Nanci. 1978. "Testimony." *Domestic Violence*, 101-110. Sacramento: California Legislature Senate Committee on Judiciary.

Corrigan, Carol. 1978. "Testimony." *Domestic Violence*, 123-137. Sacramento: California Legislature Senate Committee on Judiciary.

Davidson, Terry. 1978. *Conjugal Crime*. New York: Hawthorne Books.

de Tocqueville, Alexis. 1969. "Of Individualism in Democracies." In *Democracy in America* trans. by George Lawrence, and edited by J. P. Mayer. Vol. 2. New York: Doubleday and Company.

Dobash, R. Emerson, and Russell P. Dobash. 1979. *Violence Against Wives: The Case Against the Patriarchy.* New York: Free Press.

Douglas, Mary. 1986. *How Institutions Think.* New York: Syracuse University Press.

Ebony Magazine.
    1981. "Battered Women" (W. Leavy). February: 94-6+.

Emerson, Robert M., and Sheldon L. Messinger. 1977. "The Micro-Politics of Trouble." *Social Problems* 25 (Dec): 121-134.

Erler, Monica. 1978. "Testimony." *Battered Women: Issues of Public Policy.* Washington, D.C.: United States Commission on Civil Rights, 108-113.

Essence Magazine.
    1983. "Why Women Stay with Men Who Beat Them" (B. Mesch). April: 84-7+.
    1979. "Battered Women" (T. Breiter). June: 74-5+.

Fernandez, Shelly. 1978. "Testimony." *Battered Women: Issues of Public Policy.* Washington, D.C.: United States Commission on Civil Rights, 98-108+.

Ferraro, Kathleen. 1983. "Negotiating Trouble in a Battered Women's Shelter." *Urban Life* 12(3):287-306.

———. 1981. "Processing Battered Women." *Journal of Family Issues* 2(4):415-438.

Ferraro, Kathleen J., and John M. Johnson. 1983. "How Women Experience Battering: The Process of Victimization." *Social Problems* 30(3):325-339.

Fields, Marjory. 1978. "Testimony." *Battered Women: Issues of Public Policy.* Washington, D.C.: United States Commission on Civil Rights, 20-27.

Fine, Michelle. 1985. "Unearthing Contradictions: An Essay Inspired by Women and Male Violence." *Feminist Studies* 11(2):391-407.

Finn, Jerry. 1985. "The Stresses and Coping Behavior of Battered Women." *Social Casework* 85(6):341-349.

Fleming, Jennifer Baker. 1979. *Stopping Wife Abuse: A Guide to the Emotional, Psychological and Legal Implications for the Abused Woman and Those Helping Her*. New York: Anchor Books.

Flitcraft, Anne. 1978a. "Testimony." *Research Into Violent Behavior: Domestic Violence*. Washington, D.C.: United States Government Printing Office, 187-245.

————. 1978b. "Testimony." *Battered Women: Issues of Public Policy*. Washington, D.C.: United States Commission on Civil Rights, 113-115.

Flynn, John P. 1977. "Recent Findings Related to Wife Abuse." *Social Casework* 58(1):13-20.

Garfinkel, Harold. 1967. *Studies in Ethnomethodology*. New Jersey: Prentice-Hall.

Gelles, Richard J. 1976. "Abused Wives: Why Do They Stay?" *Journal of Marriage and the Family* 38(4):659-668.

Gelles, Richard J., and Claire Pedrick Cornell. 1985. *Intimate Violence in Families*. Beverly Hills: Sage Publications.

Gelles, Richard J., and Murray A. Straus. 1979. "Determinants of Violence in the Family: Toward a Theoretical Integration." In *Contemporary Theories About the Family, Volume 1, Research Based Theories*, edited by Wesley R. Burr, Reuben Hill, F. Ivan Nye, and Ira L. Reiss, 549-581. New York: Free Press.

Giovannoni, Jeanne M., and Rosina M. Becerra. 1979. *Defining Child Abuse*. New York: Free Press.

Glamour Magazine.
    1986. "How to Recognize a Potential Batterer" (H. Benedict). October: 206+.
    1980. "Scarred Lives of Battered Women." October: 56.

Goffman, Erving. 1961. *Asylums: Essays on the Social Situation of Mental Patients and Other Inmates*. New York: Anchor Books.

Good Housekeeping Magazine.
    1979. "I Was a Battered Wife." May: 34+.
    1976. "New Hope for the Battered Wife." August: 94-5+.

Graham, Dee L. R., Edna Rawlings, and Nelly Rimini. 1988. "Survivors of Terror: Battered Women, Hostages and the Stockholm Syndrome." In *Feminist Perspectives on Wife Abuse*, edited by Kersti Yllö and Michele Bograd, 217-233. Beverly Hills: Sage Publications.

Greenblat, Cathy Stein. 1983. "A Hit is a Hit is a Hit . . . or is it? Approval and Tolerance of the Use of Physical Force by Spouses." In *The Dark Side of Families*, edited by David Finkelhor, Richard J. Gelles, Gerald T. Hotaling, and Murray A. Straus, 235-260. Beverly Hills: Sage Publications.

Gusfield, Joseph R. 1984. "On the Side: Practical Action and Social Constructivism in Social Problems Theory." In *Studies in the Sociology of Social Problems*, edited by Joseph W. Schneider and John I. Kitsuse, 31-51. Norwood, New Jersey: Ablex Publishing.

——— . 1981. *The Culture of Public Problems: Drinking-Driving and the Symbolic Order*. Chicago: University of Chicago Press.

Hacking, Ian. 1986. "Making Up People." In *Reconstructing Individualism: Autonomy, Individuality, and the Self in Western Thought*, edited by Thomas C. Heller, Morton Sosna, and David E. Wellbery, 222-236. California: Stanford University Press.

Hanmer, Jalna, and Mary Maynard. 1987. "Introduction: Violence and Gender Stratification." In *Women, Violence and Social Control*, edited by Jalna Hanmer and Mary Maynard, 1-12. New Jersey: Humanities Press.

Hart, Barbara J. 1981. "Burn-out: A Political View." *Aegis: Magazine on Ending Violence Against Women* (Autumn): 35-40.

Herzberger, Sharon P., and Howard Tennen. 1985. "The Effect of Self-Relevance on Judgments of Moderate and Severe Disciplinary Encounters." *Journal of Marriage and the Family* 47(2):311-318.

Hilberman, Elaine. 1980. "Overview: The 'Wife-Beater's Wife' Reconsidered." *American Journal of Psychiatry* 137(11):1336-1346.

Hilberman, Elaine, and Kit Munson. 1977/1978. "Sixty Battered Women" *Victimology* 2(3-4):460-470.

Holstein, James A. 1987. "Mental Illness Assumptions in Civil Commitment Proceedings." *Journal of Contemporary Ethnography* 16(2):147-175.

Hutchins, Trova, and Vee Baxter. 1980. "Battered Women." In *Alternative*

Social Services for Women edited by Naomi Gottlieb, 179-211. New York: Columbia University Press.

Johnson, Golden. 1978. "Testimony." *Battered Women: Issues of Public Policy.* Washington, D.C.: United States Commission on Civil Rights, 54-61.

Johnson, John M. 1989. "Horror Stories and the Construction of Child Abuse." In *Images of Issues: Typifying Contemporary Social Problems* edited by Joel Best, 5-19. New York: Aldine De Gruyter.

————. 1981. "Program Enterprise and Official Cooptation in the Battered Women's Shelter Movement. *American Behavioral Scientist* 24(6):827-842.

Jones, Ann. 1980. *Women Who Kill.* New York: Holt, Rinehart and Winston.

Kalmuss, Debra. 1979. "The Attribution of Responsibility in a Wife-Abuse Context." *Victimology* 4(2):284-291.

Klein, Dorie. 1979. "Can This Marriage be Saved? Battery and Sheltering." *Crime and Social Justice* 12(winter): 19-33.

Kurz, Demie, and Evan Stark. 1988. "Not-so-Benign Neglect: The Medical Response to Battering." In *Feminist Perspectives on Wife Abuse* edited by Kersti Yllö and Michele Bograd, 249-266. Beverly Hills: Sage Publications.

Ladies Home Journal Magazine.
1985. "I Don't Want to be a Battered Wife" (J. Marks). March: 17-18+.
1979. "I Was a Battered Wife" (D. C. Disney). April: 18+.

Langley, Roger, and Richard C. Levy. 1977. *Wife Beating: The Silent Crisis.* New York: Pocket Books.

Leghorn, Lisa. 1978. "Working with Battered Women." *Victimology* 3(1,2):91-107.

Lewis, Bonnie Yegidis. 1985. "The Wife Abuse Inventory: A Screening Device for the Identification of Abused Women." Social Work 30 (1):32-35.

Lieberknecht, Kay. 1978. "Helping the Battered Wife." *American Journal of Nursing* 78(4):654-656.

Lipsky, Michael. 1980. *Street-Level Bureaucracy.* New York: Russell Sage Press.

McCalls Magazine.
  1985. "At Last We Have Hope." July: 25-8+.
  1978. "Powerless in the Suburbs: The Battered Wife" (L. Prinz). November: 63.
  1976. "Shelters for Battered Wives" (E. J. Pascoe). October: 51.

McGrath, Colleen. 1979. "The Crisis of Domestic Order." *Socialist Review* 9(1):11-30.

McLeer, Susan V. 1987. "The Role of the Emergency Physician in the Prevention of Domestic Violence." *Annals of Emergency Medicine* 16:1155-1161.

MacLeans Magazine.
  1986. "Life in a Domestic Hell" (J. Mitchell). September 22:6-7.
  1983. "Curbing the Wife-Beaters" (L. Debel). January 17:40-41.

Mademoiselle Magazine.
  1979. "On Being an Abused Wife . . . and Living in Fear" (S. Burns). December: 56+.

Martin, Del. 1979. "What Keeps a Woman Captive in a Violent Relationship? The Social Context of Battering." In *Battered Women* edited by Donna M. Moore, 33-58. Beverly Hills: Sage Publications.

————. 1976. *Battered Wives*. San Francisco: Glide Publications.

Miller, Gale, and James A. Holstein. 1989. "On the Sociology of Social Problems." In *Perspectives on Social Problems* edited by James A. Holstein and Gale Miller, 1-16. Connecticut: JAI Press.

Mills, C. Wright. 1940. "Situated Actions and Vocabularies of Motive." *American Sociological Review* 5 (Dec.): 904-913.

Mills, Trudy, and Sherryl Kleinman. 1988. "Emotions, Reflexivity and Action: An Interactional Analysis." *Social Forces* 66(4):1009-1027.

Moore, Donna M. 1979. "An Overview of the Problem." In *Battered Women* edited by Donna M. Moore, 7-32. Beverly Hills: Sage Publications.

Morgan, Patricia A. 1985. "Constructing Images of Deviance: A Look at State Intervention into the Problem of Wife-Battery." In *Marital Violence* edited by Norman Johnson, 60-76. Boston: Routledge and Kegan Paul.

————. 1981. "From Battered Wife to Program Client: The State's Shaping of Social Problems." *Kapitalistate* 9:17-40.

Morgan, Steven M. 1981. *Conjugal Terrorism: A Psychological and Community Treatment Model of Wife Abuse*. Palo Alto: R and E Associates.

Ms. Magazine.
  1979. "Northern Ireland: The Violence Isn't All in the Street" (G. Corea). July: 94+.
  1974. "London: Battered Wives" (G. Search). June: 24-26.

Murray, Susan B. 1988. "The Unhappy Marriage of Theory and Practice: An Analysis of A Battered Women's Shelter." *National Women's Studies Association Journal* 1(1):75-92.

Myers, Toby. 1978. "Testimony." *Research Into Violent Behavior: Domestic Violence*. Washington, D.C.: United States Government Printing Office, 184-185.

Nadelson, Carol, and Maria Sauzier. 1986. "Intervention Programs for Individual Victims and Their Families." In *Violence in the Home: Interdisciplinary Perspectives* edited by Mary Lystad, 153-168. New York: Brunner/Mazel, Inc.

Newberger, Eli H. 1983. "The Helping Hand Strikes Again: Unintended Consequences of Child Abuse Reporting." *Journal of Clinical Child Psychology* 12(3):307-311.

Newsweek Magazine.
  1985. "A Private Crisis, a Public Disgrace." March 11:62.

Niedemeyer, Jeannie. 1978. "Testimony." *Battered Women: Issues of Public Policy*. Washington, D.C.: United States Commission on Civil Rights, 176-178.

O'Toole, Richard, Patrick Turbett, and Claire Nalepka. 1983. "Theories, Professional Knowledge, and the Diagnosis of Child Abuse." In *The Dark Side of Families* edited by David Finkelhor, Richard J. Gelles, Gerald Hotaling, and Murray A. Straus, 349-362. Beverly Hills: Sage Publications.

Okun, Lewis. 1986. *Woman Abuse: Facts Replacing Myths*. New York: State University of New York Press.

Pagelow, Mildred Daley. 1984. *Family Violence*. New York: Praeger Publishers.

————. 1981a. *Woman-Battering: Victims and Their Experiences*. Beverly Hills: Sage Publications.

————. 1981b. "Factors Affecting Women's Decisions to Leave Violent Relationships." *Journal of Family Issues* 2(4):391-414.

Pizzey, Erin. 1979. "Pizzey Comments on American Tour." *Response* 2(7):17.

Pleck, Elizabeth. 1987. *Domestic Tyranny: The Making of American Social Policy Against Family Violence From Colonial Times to the Present.* New York: Oxford University Press.

Pleck, Elizabeth, Joseph H. Pleck, Marlyn Grossman, and Pauline Bart. 1977/1978. "The Battered Data Syndrome: A Comment on Steinmetz' Article." *Victimology* 2(3,4):680-682.

Psychology Today.
    1977. "Battered Wives Find It Hard to Get Help: Study by R. J. Gelles." June: 36+.

Ptacek, James. 1988. "Why Do Men Batter Their Wives?" In *Feminist Perspectives on Wife Abuse* edited by Kersti Yllö and Michele Bograd, 133-157. Beverly Hills: Sage Publications.

Readers Digest.
    1986. "Why Men Hurt the Women They Love" (C. Safran). January: 77-81.
    1977. "How Battered Women Can Get Help" (S. Nelson). May: 21-23+.

Redbook Magazine.
    1979. "If You Loved Me, You Wouldn't Hurt Me" (S. Edimiston). May: 99-100+.

Richardson, Deborah Capasso, and Jennifer L. Campbell. 1980. "Alcohol and Wife Abuse: The Effect of Alcohol on Atributions of Blame for Wife Abuse." *Personality and Social Psychology Bulletin* 6(1):51-56.

Richette, Lisa A. 1978. "Testimony." *Battered Women: Issues of Public Policy.* Washington, D.C.: United States Commission on Civil Rights, 128-133.

Ridington, Jillian. 1977/1978. "The Transition Process: A Feminist Environment as Reconstitutive Milieu." *Victimology* 2(3,4):563-575.

Rodriguez, Noelie Maria. 1988. "Transcending Bureaucracy: Feminist Politics at at Shelter for Battered Women." *Gender & Society* 2(2):214-227.

Romero, Mary. 1985. "A Comparison Between Strategies Used on Prisoners of

War and Battered Wives." *Sex Roles* 13(9,10):537-547.

Rossi, Peter H., Emily Waite, Christine E. Bose, and Richard E. Berk. 1974. "The Seriousness of Crimes: Normative Structure and Individual Differences." *American Sociological Review* 39(2):224-237.

Rounsaville, Bruce J. 1978. "Theories in Marital Violence: Evidence From a Study of Battered Women." *Victimology* 2(1,2):11-31.

Saunders, Daniel G. 1988. "Wife Abuse, Husband Abuse, or Mutual Combat? A Feminist Perspective on Empirical Findings." In *Feminist Perspectives on Wife Abuse* edited by Kersti Yllö and Michele Bograd, 90-113. Beverly Hills: Sage Publications.

Schechter, Susan. 1983. *Women and Male Violence: The Visions and Struggles of the Battered Women's Movement*. Boston: South End Press.

Scheuer, James H. 1978. "Comment." *Research Into Violent Behavior: Domestic Violence*. Washington, D.C.: United States Government Printing Office, 146+.

Schillinger, Elizabeth. 1988. "Dependency, Control, and Isolation: Battered Women and the Welfare System." *Journal of Contemporary Ethnography* 16(4):469-490.

Schutz, Alfred. 1970. *On Phenomenology and Social Relations*. Edited by Helmut R. Wagner. Chicago: University of Chicago Press.

————. 1962. *Collected Papers*. Edited by Arvid Brodersen. The Hague: Martinus Nijhoff.

Sedlak, Andrea J. 1988. "The Effects of Personal Experiences with Couple Violence on Calling it 'Battering' and Allocating Blame." In *Coping with Family Violence: Research and Policy Perspectives* edited by Gerald T. Hotaling, David Finkelhor, John T. Kirkpatrick, and Murray A. Straus. Beverly Hills: Sage Publications.

Segovia-Ashley, Marta. 1978a. "Testimony." *Battered Women: Issues of Public Policy*. Washington, D.C.: United States Commission on Civil Rights, 98-107.

————. 1978b. "Shelters: Short-term Needs." *Battered Women: Issues of Public Policy*. Washington, D.C.: United States Commission on Civil Rights, 371-400.

References 211

Shainess, Natalie. 1977. "Psychological Aspects of Wife Battering." In *Battered Women: A Psychosociological Study of Domestic Violence* edited by Maria Roy, 111-118. New York: Van Nostrand Rheinhold Company.

Spotted Eagle, Faith. 1978. "Testimony." *Battered Women: Issues of Public Policy.* Washington, D.C.: United States Commission on Civil Rights, 115-117.

Stark, Evan, Ann Flitcraft, and William Frazier. 1979. "Medicine and Patriarchal Violence: The Social Construction of a 'Private' Event." *International Journal of Health Services* 9(3):461-493.

Straus, Murray A., Richard J. Gelles, and Suzanne Steinmetz. 1980. *Behind Closed Doors: Violence in the American Home.* New York: Anchor Books.

Strauss, Anselm. 1978. *Negotiations: Varieties, Contexts, Processes and Social Order.* Washington: Jossey Bass Inc., Publishers.

Strube, Michael J. 1988. "The Decision to Leave an Abusive Relationship." In *Coping with Family Violence: Research and Policy Perspectives* edited by Gerald T. Hotaling, David Finkelhor, John T. Kirkpatrick, and Murray A. Straus, 93-106. Beverly Hills: Sage Publications.

Strube, Michael J., and Linda S. Barbour. 1984. "Factors Related to the Decision to Leave an Abusive Relationship." *Journal of Marriage and the Family* 46(4):837-844.

Studer, Marlena. 1984. "Wife beating as a Social Problem: The Process of Definition." *International Journal of Women's Studies* 7(Nov-Dec): 412-422.

Sullivan, Gail. 1982. "Cooptation of Alternative Services: The Battered Women's Movement as a Case Study." *Catalyst* 14(2):39-56.

Sullivan, Gail, and Jane Weiss. 1981. "How We Support Battered Women." In *For Shelter and Beyond* edited by Massachusetts Coalition of Battered Women Service Groups, 23-25. Boston: Massachusetts Coalition of Battered Women Service Groups.

Tierney, Kathleen. 1982. "The Battered Women Movement and the Creation of the Wife Beating Problem." *Social Problems* 29(3):207-217.

Time Magazine.
    1985. "A Troubled Double Life" (R. Stengel). March 11:32.
    1983. "Wife Beating: The Silent Crime" (J. O'Reilly). September 5:23-24+.

Truninger, Elizabeth. 1971. "Marital Violence: The Legal Solutions." *Hastings Law Journal* 23 (Nov): 259-276.

Turner, Susan F., and Constance Hoenk Shapiro. 1986. "Battered Women: Mourning the Death of a Relationship." *Social Work* 31(5):372-376.

United States Commission on Civil Rights. 1978. *Battered Women: Issues of Public Policy*. Washington, D.C.: United States Commission on Civil Rights.

U.S. News Magazine.
1976. "Battered Wives: Now They're Fighting Back." September 20:47-48.

Vogue Magazine.
1978. "He Beat Me" (J. B. Victor). January: 177+.

Waites, Elizabeth A. 1977/1978. "Female Masochism and the Enforced Restriction of Choice." *Victimology* 2(3,4):535-544.

Walker, Lenore. 1979. *The Battered Woman*. New York: Harper and Row.

———. 1978. "Testimony." *Research Into Violent Behavior: Domestic Violence*. Washington, D.C.: United States Government Printing Office, 145-149.

Wardell, Laurie, Dair L. Gillespie, and Ann Leffler. 1983. "Science and Violence Against Wives." In *The Dark Side of Families* edited by David Finkelhor, Richard J. Gelles, Gerald T. Hotaling, and Murray A. Straus, 69-84. Beverly Hills: Sage Publications.

Warrior, Betsy. 1978. *Working on Wife Abuse*. Cambridge, Massachusetts. 46 Pleasant Street.

Wermuth, Laurie. 1983. "Domestic Violence Reforms: Policing the Private?" *Berkeley Journal of Sociology* 27:27-49.

Wharton, Carol S. 1989. "Splintered Visions: Staff/Client Disjunctures and Their Consequences for Human Service Organizations. *Journal of Contemporary Ethnography* 19(1):50-71.

INDEX

Abusive man, collective representation: content of, 15-16, 19-20, 23, 52; and heterogeneity, 48, 50, 96, 107, 109-110

Alcohol use: and the battered woman, 27, 46, 80-81; and South Coast clients, 61, 78, 130-131

Battered woman, collective representation: as appropriate shelter client, 37-38; content of, 3, 15-16, 18, 20, 22-28, 52-53, 117-118; and heterogeneity, 39, 51, 54, 154-155; as interpretive device, 3, 90, 113, 142-143, 153-154; as mandate for social intervention, 28; and organization of shelters, 28-38, 117-118; and problem of identification, 51-53; reproduction of, 39, 93-94, 144-145, 158-165; and social problem claim viability, 46-47, 149-150. *See also* South Coast clients

Berger, Peter, 100

Child abuse, 43, 63, 149, 152-153
Clark, Candace, 45, 150

Collective representations: definition of, 3, 41; institutionalization of, 55, 69, 144; as interpretive device, 51, 98, 153-154; reproduction of, 5, 39, 40, 53, 161-165; as social problem claims, 51, 53, 149-151. *See also* Abusive man, Battered woman, Shelters, Wife abuse

Complementary oppositions, 147
Corrigan, Carol, 47

Dirty work, 104, 123
Douglas, Mary, 1, 2, 41, 53, 92, 147

Emerson, Robert, 113
Emotions work, 102-103, 106, 108, 129

Family: and the battered woman, 22-25, 175n.4; and South Coast, 58; troubles, 47-48, 54, 148-149; and wife abuse, 15, 47, 148, 156-157

Feminism: and psychological therapy, 34; at South Coast, 58, 67; and wife abuse, 2, 13, 25-26, 28, 174n.1, 176-177n.10